American Feminists

American

eminists

by

Robert E. Riegel

THE UNIVERSITY PRESS OF KANSAS

LAWRENCE · LONDON

© COPYRIGHT 1963 BY THE UNIVERSITY OF KANSAS PRESS

First Kansas Paperback edition 1968

Library of Congress Card Catalog Number 63-17010

PRINTED IN THE UNITED STATES OF AMERICA

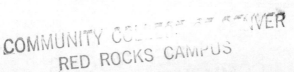

Preface

THE CHANGED POSITION of women in American society has been one of the most important developments of the past century and a half. The appearance of America has been transformed as women have invaded business, the professions, sports, politics, and education, feminizing many occupations. The American home has been altered radically with the expanded activities of women.

This change in the occupations of women has been credited frequently to the Industrial Revolution, which freed women from a portion of their household work, provided opportunities for employment, and furnished the surplus wealth to permit many new activities. This analysis has the drawback that the earliest advocates of greater rights for women appeared before the Industrial Revolution had any important impact, and apparently were only slightly if at all aware of any such event. If the pioneers had significance, then factors other than economic changes were involved. Apparently there were two interdependent lines of development, occurring to a considerable extent at the same time. One was the ideological approach, which derived directly from the ideas of the Enlightenment, and which was of prime importance to the first feminists. The other was the economic changes that made possible in fact the objectives for which the feminists fought.

The first American feminists, like the harbingers of any important change, were greeted with suspicion and hostility by the vast conservative majority, which felt dire forebodings as to the effects of the new doctrines on the American family, and in fact on all American civilization. These conservatives may well have been wrong, as we have come later to believe, but their point of view is understandable, and they performed a service in forcing the reformers to justify their claims, in making the changes evolutionary rather than revolutionary, and in eliminating some of the crackpot fringes.

Pioneers normally have not only bitterly critical opponents but also unquestioning adulators. If the cause later wins, its advocates are lauded as intelligent, far-seeing people who have conquered a stupid majority with the power of truth. If it loses, as, for example, with phrenology and anarchism, the pioneers appear later as credulous crackpots. Since feminism won, its early propagandists are now hailed as intelligent, far-seeing individuals, who presented logically uncontrovertable arguments, and who fought the prejudices of men trying selfishly to retain their preferred position in society.

The usual glorified picture of early feminists needs modification. Feminists were generally intelligent, but they were not without limitations. They were at times emotional rather than logical, they sometimes embraced unreasonable ideas, they had their jealousies and disagreements, and in fact were entirely human. Early feminists cannot properly be described as the leaders of a women's crusade against the cruelty of man. Most people, both men and women, considered incredible the idea that women were mistreated, and the ranks of reformers and conservatives included both sexes in somewhat equal numbers. The influence of the feminist arguments is an open question, but probably only accelerated a process that would have occurred in any case.

Feminists, like other fighters for unpopular causes, were unusual people. The great majority of the United States thought that women were extremely well treated, and among the minority who held the opposite point of view hardly any were willing to carry on a crusade. This book tries to describe a sufficient number of pioneer feminists to furnish the basis for at least some conclusions about the factors that produced a crusader, with the thought that statements about any one group of "hopeful martyrs" may throw light on others fighting for different causes.

The following descriptions and generalizations have several consciously adopted limitations. Only women have been included for extended discussion, since feminism was for most male reformers only a secondary interest. Among these women are most of the better-known feminists, but certain exclusions seemed desirable. Women whose primary interest was in some other field, such as medicine or social work, have not been included even if they were devoted feminists; in some cases such exclusions may seem questionable, as do certain inclusions. An occasional cause of exclusion has been such paucity of material that any analysis would be unreliable. Even with these ground rules, problems still remain. Available material is sometimes rich and sometimes scanty, is usually tinged strongly with emotional distortion, and is frequently least full at exactly the points of greatest interest. Never to be forgotten are the personal limitations of the author, who at the best has only one life to devote to a subject, however fascinating.

My gratitude to many people is almost infinite. Librarians have not only been uniformly courteous and well informed, but have usually been helpful far beyond the call of duty. I am particularly grateful to the following libraries and their fine staffs: Boston Public, New York Public, Library of Congress, New York State, New York State Historical, Syracuse University, University of Rochester, Seneca Falls Historical Society, Huntington, Massachusetts Historical, Wisconsin Historical, Cornell Collection of Regional History, American Antiquarian, Columbia University. The Dartmouth Library has of course been used extensively, and I have an unpayable debt to its excellent staff. The largest collections of material dealing with women are the Sophia Smith Collection of Smith College and the Women's Archives of Radcliffe; working in them with the help of their friendly staffs is a sheer delight. Among individuals who have been helpful I would like to express my special appreciation to Professor Jewel Bellush of Hunter College, Professor Bernard Bellush of City College of

New York, and Mr. Harry Scheiber of Dartmouth College, who read the entire manuscript. Professor Thomas Le Duc of Oberlin College and Professor Allen Kifer of Skidmore College gave much appreciated advice. Miss Eleanor Flexner has also been very helpful, both personally and by her writings. I am also thankful to the John Simon Guggenheim Foundation for a grant that has permitted much work that might otherwise have been impossible. Finally, I am as usual grateful to my wife Mabel C. Riegel, who has participated actively both in gathering and in interpreting the material.

ROBERT E. RIEGEL

Dartmouth College
December 8, 1962

Contents

1
First Stirrings

AN AMERICAN GIRL of the early nineteenth century looked forward to a predictable and well-ordered life. She could expect an elementary education at least as good as that of her brother, but no advanced study except possibly a period in finishing school if her family was sufficiently wealthy. She was faced with no decision as to whether she would train to be a nurse, a secretary, a librarian, a biochemist, or a dentist, since such occupations either did not exist or were not open to women. Her training was designed to enable her to catch her man and to provide the necessary elementary information for a housewife.

After completing her schooling, the girl expected to stay home and help her mother with the housework and with the care of younger children. In some ways this period was the most enjoyable of her life. Though she worked fairly hard she had little responsibility, and found time to make attractive clothes, to giggle and gossip with her girl friends, to attend parties, and to flirt with the adolescent boys. Her one real worry was to attract a proper husband, for she knew that here was the usual measure of her success in life, and that her future status in society depended primarily upon that of her husband. The fiction that the male pursued the shrinking and elusive female was only a pleasant substitution for the real facts.

Marriage was the greatest single moment of a girl's life, with the possible exception of the birth of her first child, and was both a sad and a joyful event. The sadness came from the realization that a carefree and happy girlhood was giving way to the cares and responsibilities of adult life. The happiness came from the prospective consummation of her love, the ex-

1

pectation of a family of her own, and the security and social acceptability of her new status as a married woman. A woman realized that delay of marriage for even a few years would lower her prestige in the community, since then she would be labeled as an old maid, with a living to earn by such undesirable occupations as trimming hats, going from house to house to sew for critical and parsimonious wives, or acting as an unpaid drudge in the home of a married brother or sister. The worst of such a way of life would be the pity and condescension of her community.

As a wife, the woman of the early nineteenth century had fairly certain prospects. Living ordinarily on a farm, she expected to do all of the housework for a growing family. She controlled preparation of food from garden to table, and clothes from the raw material to the finished product; she made soap and candles, washed the clothes, scrubbed the floor, and performed all the other tasks of a non-mechanized home. If she was sufficiently fortunate to live in town and to be well-to-do, she might have servants and be able to devote more time to fancy sewing and social activities. No matter what her status, however, children soon appeared in regular procession. Births were usually in the home, with no more than the care of a neighboring wife or midwife, and the mortality rate was pathetically high. Laments on the deaths of loved children were omnipresent in the magazines, and were well justified by the facts.

The satisfactions of married life for the woman depended largely on the adequacy of her husband, just as his happiness depended in considerable part upon his wife. In the early nineteenth century, as in any other period, there were husbands who were penurious, bad-tempered, cruel, thoughtless, drunken, and unsuccessful, and there were wives who were frivolous, slatternly, extravagant, lazy, sharp-tongued—perhaps poor cooks and bad managers. The result was unhappy marriages, fortunately rare. Foreign observers always spoke enthusiastically about the happiness of American marriage.

In later years, the more ardent feminists were to contend that wives were generally dissatisfied because they were enslaved under the common law, subject to the whims of their husbands and without rights of their own. This contention represented the compounding of several errors. American states had generally adopted the English common law as interpreted by Blackstone, and the first mistake was the failure to realize that Blackstone as an unyielding conservative had misstated the legal situation in England. The second mistake was in not recognizing that the Blackstone principles concerning women had been vastly modified in the United States by statute law, by equity law, and by the use of pre- and postnuptial agreements. The third error was to assume that the most objectionable of the Blackstone ideas were quite generally put into effect. Women were in fact far from the slaves that the feminists depicted with their quotations from Blackstone. Mrs. Mary Beard, our best investigator of the subject, and herself an ardent supporter of woman's rights, has gone so far as to state that "the dogma of woman's complete historic subjection to man must be rated as one of the most fantastic myths ever created by the human mind."[1]

The real dependence of a wife on her husband was based on causes other than legal. The husband provided the family income, which meant the difference between affluence and penury. The husband's profession was the prime source of his family's status in the community. He made the public appearances and held the honorary offices in all outside organizations, including the government. In a very real sense the husband was the dominant partner, even though the picture of him as a tyrant backed by man-made law was fantastic.

The normal division of functions between men and women was reasonable in terms of existing conditions. A woman quite normally and properly expected to get married, and the duties

3

of marriage would preclude many activities outside the home. Her quarter century devoted largely to pregnancy, childbirth, and the nursing of babies contained little spare time for the woman of average strength to direct the local temperance society or to run for the state legislature. Society found few surplus funds to waste in teaching a girl such extraneous matters as Latin, Greek, and calculus, and why should a girl be trained as a scientist or philosopher? As to her working outside the home, there were few available jobs in a non-mechanized world, and as a wife she had little time for even those few. Women without husbands represented a real problem requiring special solutions, but constituted a minority situation. Little wonder that the overwhelming majority of both men and women accepted the normal division between men's and women's work as not only inevitable but also desirable.

A differentiation in the functions of the sexes naturally brought obvious differences in mental and emotional reactions, which in turn inspired speculations as to whether women were inherently different from men in intellect and emotions. The majority opinion was that women were endowed with less strength of mind than men, just as they had less strength of body, though there were vigorous dissents. A few radicals contended that native endowments were equal, and urged that women be given more educational opportunities so that regardless of their special occupations they could meet men on equal intellectual terms. The difference of opinion was basically the ever-existing argument of nature versus nurture. Everyone agreed that differences existed, but they argued whether the differences were inherent and produced the separate fields of interest, or whether the separate fields of interest produced the differences.

Majority opinion held that, regardless of total intellectual capacity, women had innate and important mental peculiarities. Women were felt to arrive at conclusions more by intuition than by logic, and to be unable to grasp the higher realms of advanced mathematics, governmental theory, and philosophy. Such an assumption of course implied the exclusion of women from numerous occupations. While no one was so silly as to hold that no woman could reason effectively and that every man was a potential philosopher, the division of abilities was considered as sufficiently well marked to be the basis of action.

Women were held to be generally more pure, delicate, good, and spiritual than men. Gross physical passions, including not only sex but the more violent emotions such as are associated with hate, revenge, and aggressiveness, were considered more male than female. Seldom, in popular opinion, could a woman qualify as either a Don Juan or a Napoleon. The woman reflected more passive virtues, like philanthropy, self-abnegation, and the love of God. Worship of the Most High was transmitted by inheritance and precept from a mother to her children. In fact, woman's most glorious function was to bear children and to instill in them the pure Christian faith and morals which were among the greatest glories of American society.

Women were above all innately delicate and modest, which meant much more than clothing their bodies carefully, or even than guarding their reading, amusements, actions, and speech. Women in general should cling to the isolated sanctity of the home, thus avoiding the degradation coming from too great contact with gross men. Certainly they should not be clerks or sailors or physicians, and likewise they should not appear on public platforms, particularly before mixed audiences, and should not hold positions which caused them to preside over large groups. If a woman unfortunately had no husband and was forced to earn her own living, her best job was one which minimized her contact with men, as for example dressmaking, or hat-making, or even working with other girls in a mill. Here and there a woman, even in colonial days, had run a farm or business, but she had generally been a widow who merely carried on the work of her late husband, and as normal activities such occupations were considered highly undesirable.

The vast majority of women accepted this analysis of feminine characteristics as valid, and felt no desire to protest against the limitation of their activities. Their minds had been conditioned by quantities of argument from pulpit and press, and the idea probably never occurred to them that they might compete effectively with men in occupations normally monopolized by males. The only important exceptions were teaching and writing. A woman might with propriety teach, even after marriage, and the earlier male monopoly of the profession was being broken, particularly in the lower grades. Writing was also socially acceptable, although generally confined to didactic novels, children's stories, cookbooks, missionary memoirs, and other non-controversial material. A woman might even sign her own name without accusations of immodesty, although many women authors continued to use pseudonyms. But, with such exceptions, women held to their commonly approved place in society. No doubt individuals were at times maladjusted, but the answer was that no institution can be arranged to be adapted perfectly to exceptional cases, and it was felt that in general unusual individuals should adjust themselves to the society in which they lived. Sinners should be saved, rather than having their sins made an acceptable way of life.

Here and there exceptional people refused to conform to the traditional ideas of the society in which they lived, objecting bitterly to the circumscribed opportunities of women:

> How wretched is poor woman's fate!
> No happy change her fortune knows;
> Subject to man in ev'ry state,
> How can she then be free from woes?[2]

These protesters have later been unearthed and acclaimed as prophets, which they may have been, but with no recognition that a fair proportion were men. Mr. and Mrs. John Adams

6

are a good example. Abigail Adams' plea to "remember the ladies and be more generous and favorable to them than were your ancestors"[3] has been cited frequently and approvingly as a general plea for female equality, which it was not; the concern was with the rights of married women. What is almost always forgotten is that the husband, John Adams, was at least as reform-minded as his wife. In general he favored the equality of the sexes, and once proposed that women be permitted to vote, although usually he did not approve of the participation of women in politics.

The first ardent and prominent American feminist was actually a man—the novelist Charles Brockden Brown. His book *Alcuin: A Dialogue of the Rights of Women* (1796-97) was the first American book to be devoted to propagandizing the rights of women.[4] In it the awkward, priggish, and self-conscious schoolmaster Alcuin carries on a long and dull discussion with the brilliant Philadelphia socialite, Mrs. Elizabeth Carter, in which women are described as the equals of men except in morality, where they are superior. Ultimately Alcuin outlines a future utopia in which women wear the same clothes as men and enter the same occupations, in which marriage is based on reason rather than on emotion, and in which divorce is easy. These extreme views might have aroused a considerable storm if the book had not been so dull that almost no one read it. Any real effect of the Brown views came from their appearance in several later novels.

The first feministic book by an American woman was written by Hannah Mather Crocker and appeared in 1818. It bore the intimidating and descriptive title of *Observations on the Real Rights of Women, with Their Appropriate Duties, Agreeable to Scripture, Reason and Common Sense*. Obviously the author was not counting on sales which depended on catching the eye of a passenger hurrying to change stage-coaches. But then Mrs. Crocker would have rejected indignantly any effort to attract sales by popularization. After all,

7

she was bathed in extraordinary amounts of piety, even for New England. Her grandfather was the redoubtable Cotton Mather, and she was literally surrounded by ministers, including her father, her husband, and her husband's father. She bore a total of ten children in rapid succession, but apparently with worse physical effects on her husband than on herself; at least he died moderately young, though she lived to the age of seventy-nine. The old story of the wife harried to the grave by excessive childbearing, while her husband took a second or even a third wife, was certainly not illustrated by Mrs. Crocker. Her writing started after her husband's death—a sequence of events which was not unusual.

Mrs. Crocker's book is disappointing to anyone looking for feministic radicalism. Mrs. Crocker accepted the ordinary assumption that Eve and her daughters had been made subservient to men because of Eve's sin, although she contended that Adam was not entirely blameless in regard to the forbidden fruit. She argued that women had as much intellectual ability as men, with equal power to distinguish between right and wrong, and that they had been restored to grace with the beginning of the Christian dispensation. This argument in behalf of women might logically have been applied to every phase of life, but Mrs. Crocker confined herself to advocating the equality of mother and father in the home. She accepted the different activities of men and women outside the home, merely arguing that each sex should seek to do its best in its own sphere.

These early American feministic doctrines created scarcely a ripple of excitement and hence produced little effect. Mrs. Crocker's only radicalism was the proposal of equality within the family, basically a matter of individual adjustment. Charles Brockden Brown's dialogue probably had its greatest utility as a soporific, while its ideas had not even the virtue of originality, since they were drawn largely from the Englishwoman Mary Wollstonecraft, whose writings were far more influential than those of any American of the period. Probably it is only natural that American feminism, like so many other reforms, drew heavily on English sources.

The Wollstonecraft views had been presented in her book, *A Vindication of the Rights of Women* (1792), soon reprinted in the United States. This volume furnished many of the arguments and points of view which later American feminists were to broadcast. Quite apparently it was the heartfelt expression of a woman who had experienced the heights and depths of emotion. Unfortunately, however, it was poorly written, badly arranged, and repetitious. Undoubtedly it pleased greatly a few readers with similar beliefs; Lucretia Mott, for example, called it "my pet book."[5] But most Americans were shocked, and felt the book to be both "singular and reprehensible."[6] One can well argue that the Wollstonecraft emotionalism and radicalism did more to anger and antagonize than to persuade.

Mary Wollstonecraft aimed passionate blows at the customary double standard of morals, holding that men and women should adhere to the same definitions of virtue: "I . . . deny the existence of sexual virtue, not excepting modesty."[7] She protested bitterly at the superiority assumed by men: "I lament that women are systematically degraded by receiving the trivial attentions which men think it manly to pay to the sex, when, in fact, they are insultingly supporting their own superiority."[8] Within marriage the partners should feel equally free to express their natural emotions. All too frequently, Miss Wollstonecraft thought, women "feign an unnatural coldness of constitution"[9] as a means of spurring male interest and excitement in the conquest. Women, she held, had strong sexual impulses, and "women as well as men ought to have the common appetites and passions of their nature."[10]

The Wollstonecraft plan of improvement was to have women given better education, both mental and physical, so that they could meet men on more nearly a basis of equality. Her emphasis was on the personal relations of the sexes, especially the physical. She avoided completely the comparative mental ability of the sexes, and was little concerned with the opportunities for women outside the home. By implication she accepted the existing differences in the activities of the sexes.

Mary Wollstonecraft shocked most Americans deeply. Her book spoke quite frankly of the physical passions of marriage at a time when the subject was not mentioned in print except in the most vague and flowery, and often incomprehensible, language. Even worse, she asserted the existence of strong sexual passions in women at a time when the popular assumption was that pure women, which meant practically all women, were almost sexless, and only endured sexual embraces from love of their mates and from the desire for children.

Quite commonly, Americans threw up their hands and shuddered, holding that such views would break down proper morality and destroy the family. And then they discovered that Miss Wollstonecraft's own life illustrated their worst fears. While they could sympathize with her girlhood, during which a drunken and shiftless father had caused his daughters to fend for themselves, they could hardly condone the fact that Miss Wollstonecraft had lived with two men without the formality of marriage. These lapses from current morality had occurred after Miss Wollstonecraft published her book but before many Americans had read it. Her first male consort was the American artist Gilbert Imlay, with whom she traveled over Europe, and by whom she bore a daughter. Her second venture was with the English social philosopher William Godwin, who finally made an "honest woman" of her to legitimize their child, even though he did not believe in marriage. For most Americans here was proof that the Wollstonecraft views led to social disorganization and immorality, while her death in bearing her second child indicated the disapproval of God.

The first really articulate feminist to display herself in person to the American public was another Englishwoman (more accurately, Scottish), Frances Wright, known commonly as

Fanny. Frances Wright's father had been something of a radical, but there is no significance in this fact, since both of Fanny's parents died when she was two, and she was reared by relatives in London. Frances was prosperous, well educated, and personally attractive; she was full of new ideas and had the energy to express them. At the age of eighteen she left her foster home, and a few years later she and her younger sister Camilla visited the United States—a daring act for two unchaperoned young ladies in 1818. The high point of the trip was the production in New York of a play written by Frances; unhappily, it was a failure.

The sisters returned to America in 1824, and this time stayed six years. Frances devoted the early part of the visit to traveling with Lafayette, then making a triumphal tour of the nation he had helped to establish. According to her friend Robert Dale Owen, Frances Wright was attractive.[11] Tall, slender, and graceful, she had a clear-cut profile which Owen thought a trifle masculine but to which others reacted differently. Her forehead was low, and broad. Short, curly chestnut hair clung to her head. Large, earnest blue eyes dominated her face. Her clothes tended to be simple, as of white muslin, and at times she wore Quaker costume. Her mind was well stored with a great diversity of knowledge, and her thinking was clear and logical provided one accepted her basic assumptions. She spoke clearly and effectively, whether in private conversation or in public orations.

Frances Wright's basic belief was in freedom and equality for all people, and in the service of this ideal she gave the complete devotion of an intensely passionate nature. She attacked ardently the limitations which she felt to be inherent in private property, irrational religion, and traditional marriage. She fought for equal rights for all, regardless of wealth, social status, sex, nation, or race. In these ideas she was in general accord with the beliefs of the Scottish industrialist Robert Owen, whose utopian community of New Harmony,

11

Indiana, she visited. Rather curiously, Owen had been influenced considerably by Percy Bysshe Shelley, who in turn had been influenced by Godwin and had married the daughter of Godwin and Mary Wollstonecraft. Miss Wright was a particularly good friend of Robert Owen's son Robert Dale Owen, and the two worked together in various projects, including most notably the publication of the *Free Enquirer* (New York), a paper which sponsored all sorts of reforms, with emphasis on the advance of the laboring classes.

Within this context of a general belief in freedom and equality, the ideas of Miss Wright about women almost define themselves. Women should have complete freedom of action, with equality in education, employment, marriage, and every other sphere. These ideals were put into at least partial practice in a model community established by Miss Wright in 1826 at Nashoba, near Memphis. Originally this community had been designed to train Negroes for freedom, and as such had the blessings of Madison, Monroe, and Jefferson, but it soon admitted whites as well as Negroes, and adopted various utopian principles. Private ownership of property was abolished, with trustees holding the necessary land titles. Religion was frowned upon. Sexual arrangements were to be the free choice of the parties concerned, to be terminated when they wished. The number of children was to be limited, and their care a community enterprise.

Miss Wright's exact attitude toward marriage remains a trifle obscure. Her statement about Nashoba read: "The marriage law existing without the pale of the institution (Nashoba) is of no force within that pale. No woman can forfeit her individual rights or independent existence, and no man assert over her any rights or power whatsoever beyond what he may exercise over her free and voluntary affection."[12] The reasonable implication that marriage as a legal form was being abolished received corroboration from the actions of her sister Camilla. Camilla actually was married at Nashoba, but then

12

wrote in the community journal an apology for the act, explaining that the prejudice of neighbors was so great that she did not care to risk the strong disapprobation that would result if she were not married. Apparently one of the great hopes of the Nashoba experiment was that free sexual union would in time result in the amalgamation of the white and colored races, and consequently end the racial problem once and forever. Later in life Miss Wright contended that she had never opposed the institution of marriage, but this statement may possibly have been disingenuous. Very easy divorce would have produced approximately the same results as the elimination of the marriage ceremony.

The extent to which Frances Wright exemplified her own theories of sexual freedom cannot be stated with accuracy. Undoubtedly she was a passionate woman with many love affairs, including some with men like Byron whom she never met. At this late date her exact involvements cannot be determined. Mention has been made of her friendship with Robert Dale Owen, but he insisted later that the attraction was entirely platonic—mental and not physical. Much speculation has occurred about her relations to Lafayette, in whose home she lived for a considerable time; whether the elderly Lafayette thought of her as a daughter, or a protégée, or in some other role is uncertain. Miss Wright was finally married as she approached her thirty-sixth birthday, but she took this drastic action only upon the near advent of a child—a daughter, Sylvia. Her husband was one William Phiquepal D'Arusmont, whom she met in New Harmony, where he had been teaching school, and who was described as an ugly, vain, virile little Frenchman, possibly something of a genius, but certainly impossible to domesticate properly. The marriage was far from happy, ending in divorce.

The failure of the Nashoba community did nothing to lessen Miss Wright's confidence in the correctness of her views. She expressed them in the *Free Enquirer,* and dilated on them at length in speeches throughout the country. Everywhere she appeared she was greeted by large crowds, including many women. Possibly they were impressed by her message, but more likely they were attracted by her notoriety. Usually the audiences were quiet and appreciative, but at times they were turbulent and hostile. Philadelphia seemed the most troublesome place, with difficulty in obtaining a hall, confusion in the audience, and finally a deathlike silence from the newspapers.

The apparently sympathetic reception of the Wright speeches was a tribute to the tolerance of the American public and to the personal attractiveness of Fanny Wright. Miss Wright's tall and commanding appearance, her clear-cut features, and her eloquence tended to dominate her audiences. But her message attacked the most basic beliefs of Americans— private property, the authority of the Christian religion, and the sanctity of marriage; she even went so far as to propose that illegitimate children be treated like the offspring of legal marriages. Americans could hardly accept such ideas as within the sphere of legitimate action, but, led by the newspapers, usually were willing to listen quietly.[13]

The reactions of Americans were in fact almost universally hostile. Miss Wright was labeled "the Red Harlot of Infidelity,"[14] a "female Tom Paine" trying to "subvert our fundamental principles of morality"[15] and showing "a monstrous depravity of heart" and a "fatal fanaticism which has absorbed and swallowed up every feeling of delicacy, the inseparable characteristics of American females."[16] She constituted, according to the critics, a "disgusting exhibition of female impudence"[17] as she tried to convince Americans "that *religion* is a cheat, *chastity* a dream, and all who adhere to the pure precepts of the gospel of our Saviour, fools!"[18] Quite clearly, American tolerance did not involve an acceptance of the Wright doctrines.

These first gropings toward feminism were little more than slight hints of the future. Suggestions of dissatisfaction with the place of women in American society were but a few harmless clouds in an otherwise clear sky. Possibly worth noting is the fact that the feminist propagandists to date were people of superior wealth, education, and social status. The most active and radical of them, Frances Wright, was a spectacularly unusual person. Whether she did more to help or to damage the cause may be argued, but certainly there was no significant feminist movement apparent at the end of her work. Any effective domestic agitation would of necessity be somewhat more conservative than hers, and related more directly and practically to the American background and conditions of life.

2
Lady Reformers

A VIGOROUS and active-minded woman of the early nineteenth century was sometimes not content to confine her interest and labor to her husband and children. Her surplus energies found their most easily available and socially approved outlet in some kind of charitable or religious work, since everyone assumed that women are soft-hearted, humane, and pious, with deep sympathy for unfortunates and strong religious leanings. A lady could easily find outlets in such obvious activities as decorating the pastor's study, carrying baskets to the poor, sewing for missionaries, or taking flowers to the sick. On a slightly more impersonal basis she might work in one of the many philanthropic movements of the period. She might attend inspirational meetings, and help to raise funds, as by a bazaar, for such good causes as consoling prisoners, reforming prostitutes, helping the aged, or providing for widows. Greatest sentimental interest seemed to go to orphans, partly because Americans idolized children, and partly because orphans were more eligible for salvation than other, and older, classes of unfortunates.

Instead of using her spare time in alleviating suffering, the energetic lady might harness her enthusiasm in support of one of the many crusades designed to improve society and thus lessen the number of the unfortunates. Such reforms were almost infinite in variety, with such aims as eliminating the use of tobacco, obtaining proper observance of the Sabbath, expanding foreign or domestic missions, encouraging proper dress, and suppressing undesirable books, plays, pictures, and statues. Working for any such cause had general social ap-

17

proval, provided the lady did not unduly neglect her family or push herself too blatantly before the public.

The most important reform movements, if importance may be judged by enthusiasm, were temperance and abolition. Temperance was considered particularly fitting for the woman reformer because of the theory—not always supported by fact—that women always and quite properly opposed the use of liquor. When feminism developed, every feminist was a supporter of temperance, even though by no means all temperance advocates were feminists. A standard wail of the believers in women's rights was the mistreatment by drunken husbands of their faithful and suffering wives.

Abolition was a less universally approved activity for women than temperance, since slavery was supported by many women as well as by men, and by Northerners as well as by Southerners. In many cases women working for abolition were not greeted even with tolerance. Just like their male companions in arms, such as Gerrit Smith, Theodore Weld, William Lloyd Garrison, and the Tappan brothers, they walked a thorny path. In addition to the normal opposition incited by any Abolitionist, the ladies had to meet a special hostility as women, particularly when they did public speaking, and this hostility was extremely influential in creating feminists.

The tendency to link abolition and feminism was a distinctly limiting factor for feminism. Whereas the temperance movement attracted women from all over the country, abolition had its appeal only to Northern women, the Southern ladies by and large accepting the "peculiar institution." The result was that of the many feminists who started as Abolitionists, the number of Southern women was very small, including mainly Southern-born girls such as the Grimké sisters and Lillie Devereux Blake, who spent most of their lives in the North. The general scarcity of avowed feminists in the South was further reinforced by the Southern concept of the family, extremely paternalistic, and also by the slowness of the South in becoming industrialized. In consequence the South produced very few of the early feminists.

The dean of the women who followed the path from abolition to feminism was unquestionably Lucretia Mott. Mrs. Mott's importance was so great that she has been credited by one competent author with the real origin of American feminism.[1] This characterization came not because she was the first American feminist, which she was not, but because of her invaluable services in creating an organized and cohesive movement, and because of her influence upon other women reformers—above all on that outstanding leader Elizabeth Cady Stanton. The influence of Mrs. Mott was based on a combination of appearance, temperament, and intelligence. In appearance she was small and slender, with dark hair and eyes; she remained attractive even in later years when her features sharpened with age. Her mind was clear, logical, and keen. Her manner was quiet and dignified, and her speeches were generally calmly reasonable, with none of the ranting and vituperation altogether too common. She seldom used the sarcasm that was so prevalent with her co-workers; her nearest approach was a sort of gentle raillery.

Lucretia Mott was born to the Quaker family of Coffin on Nantucket Island on January 3, 1793, a fact that made her considerably older than the women with whom she later worked for feminism. Her father was a sea captain, who moved to Boston when Lucretia was eleven. While the family fortunes collapsed for a time, there is no evidence that Lucretia suffered any serious deprivations, or indeed that she had any extraordinary formative experiences during girlhood. After a reasonably good education for the period, she started to teach school, where she fell in love with a fellow teacher, James Mott. They were married when Lucretia was eighteen; by this time James was working for his wife's father.

The married life of the Motts was extremely happy. James was quiet, thoughtful, conscientious, hard-working, and introspective, while Lucretia was more effervescent and adventurous. The couple had six children, of whom one died as a baby. Mrs. Mott was an excellent and devoted housewife. She was industrious, efficient, loving, and economical, weaving rags into carpets, and writing many of her letters on odd scraps of paper, to the distress of the modern researcher. She wrote voluminously to friends and relatives, and her gossipy letters were filled with births, sicknesses, deaths, washing, ironing, cooking, marketing, entertaining, and the other incidents of a full domestic life.

The one admirable trait that both Motts failed to exhibit was humor. They took life very seriously, with particular attention to the virtues and importance of religion. They were Quakers, but they followed the reform doctrines of Elias Hicks, who was unitarian and favored simplified living and church forms. They felt certain that their own religion was "rational," whereas others frequently exhibited "the appendages of bigoted sectarianism, and gloomy superstition!"[2] Mrs. Mott became even more intensely religious after the death of an infant son (1817), and during the following year began to speak in meetings. This experience in speaking was an advantage she had in being a Quaker, since all of the larger religious denominations discouraged women from speaking in church.

Both James and Lucretia Mott felt that their moral obligations went much further than attending church and living blameless lives. They felt a real and deep obligation to aid in the regeneration of more benighted members of society. Above all, they worked for the freedom of the slave, their main interest through the Civil War period. The intensity of their feelings received eloquent testimony when they risked their entire economic future to back their beliefs with action. James gave up his cotton business in Boston (1830) because of the connection of cotton with slavery and entered the wool trade, moving to Philadelphia, where the Motts made their home for the remainder of their lives. The greatness of the gamble is evident from the fact that the Motts had four small children at the time. Fortunately, the change was profitable, and the Motts were soon moderately well-to-do.

Since the time when Mrs. Mott became interested in feminism is uncertain, it is difficult to explain the basic reasons for her attitude. Rather late in life she wrote: "I grew up so thoroughly imbued with women's rights that it was the most important question of my life from a very early day,"[3] but this attitude seems a later rationalization. There is no contemporary evidence that she had strong feministic beliefs either in her girlhood or in her early married life, and her actions point to abolition as the dominant early interest. As she attended more and more abolition meetings she was irritated increasingly by finding herself and other women pushed into the background by males who monopolized the spotlight and expected women to limit themselves to comprising the admiring audience and to doing the hard, detailed work. She expressed her resentment to her co-worker Abby Kelley by writing: "I should be very glad if women generally and men too, could so lose sight of distinctions of sex as to act in public meetings on the enlightened and true ground of Christian equality."[4] Her protest at the treatment of women went so far as to lead her to castigate the small distinctions between the sexes that existed in Quaker meetings.

The really decisive factor in Mrs. Mott's acceptance of feminism, and in fact in the total development of the American woman's rights movement, was a world antislavery convention held at London in 1840. Several American women, including Mrs. Mott, attended as delegates, which so horrified Englishmen of traditional beliefs that after a long and acrimonious argument they relegated the women to the balcony; William Lloyd Garrison battled vigorously for the rights of the women delegates, and ultimately joined them in the balcony. Mrs. Mott did not herself participate in the argument, and later

21

she explained that "I have sometimes shrunk from a defense of our rights"[5] because she did not like to embrace unnecessary trouble.

The London experience was important not only because of the effect on Mrs. Mott, but even more because it was in this context that the young bride, Elizabeth Cady Stanton, first met the older Mrs. Mott (then forty-seven) and came under her spell. Later, Mrs. Stanton wrote: "Mrs. Mott was to me an entirely new revelation of womanhood. I sought every opportunity to be at her side, and continually plied her with questions, and I shall never cease to be grateful for the patience and seeming pleasure, with which she fed my hungering soul."[6] It was only natural that when Mrs. Stanton planned her woman's rights convention at Seneca Falls in 1848 she should invite Mrs. Mott to be a sponsor, and it was equally natural that James Mott, who agreed with his wife's ideas, should preside at the meeting.

Mrs. Mott's views concerning women and their proper place in society were not so extreme as those of most feminists.[7] She held that God had created man and woman as equals, but that woman had been limited to an inadequate sphere by "corrupt custom and a perverted application of the Scriptures."[8] Equality did not mean identity. The sexes had different characteristics and abilities, and Mrs. Mott was more kindly to the opposite sex than many of her co-workers, rejecting the frequent contention that women were superior, particularly in morals. As to male suppression of the female, she contended that either sex would be tyrannical if given the opportunity.

While Mrs. Mott accepted sex differences, she was sure that the present spheres of men and women were defined incorrectly, and that women had more varied capacities than those with which they were ordinarily credited. Women should be treated by men less as toys and more as partners in the running of the world. They should have better education. They should have greater opportunities, although in political matters Mrs.

22

Mott was more interested in legal rights than in the vote. Widened horizons would permit women to become more distinct and positive personalities, but would not lessen their femininity or distract them from their domestic duties, and here Mrs. Mott could cite her own life as proof. Above all, the added opportunities for women represented basic rights and not privileges. "Rights are not dependent upon equality of mind; nor do we admit inferiority, leaving that question to be settled by future developments, when a fair opportunity shall be given for the equal cultivation of the intellect."[9]

Mrs. Mott remained active in feminism until near her death in 1880, even though her influence lessened as her physical strength declined. Usually she was lauded by other feminists as one of the great prophets and ground-breakers, a saintly person to be revered. Any meeting was felt to be destined for almost certain success if Mrs. Mott could be persuaded to preside. Now and then, however, some younger women would resent the dominance of Mrs. Mott. Paulina Wright Davis wrote to Caroline Dall as early as 1853 that "L. Mott is in her dotage; in the chair she is full of partiality and I was about to say meanness. She absorbs all the time and gives no high character to it, she talks just the same things she has said for twenty years and in a way not suited to the present aspect of things."[10] But such an opinion was exceptional. Most people found Mrs. Mott attractive in appearance and effective in speech. Her temperate presentations were received with remarkably few protests even from people who opposed her general point of view. Her optimism appealed to Americans generally. She held that "the intelligence of the age is ripe for the woman question, and it only needs the *asking* on the part of women, to receive,"[11] while such irritating issues as free love would be only passing troubles. She occupied a very special and important place in the history of American feminism.

The eminence of Lucretia Mott threw the career of her sister Martha C. Wright into the shadow, which apparently was quite satisfactory to the sister, who seemingly had no desire for the spotlight. Mrs. Wright knew and corresponded with all the well-known feminists of her day, attended numerous conventions and presided over some of them, and was highly respected by her co-workers for her sound judgment, but she gave relatively few speeches and wrote little for publication, with the result that she was not among the well-known women of her day. Her influence, however, was widespread and important.

Martha Coffin Wright was thirteen years younger than her sister Lucretia Mott, and her letters create the image of a kindly, generous, understanding, tolerant, and home-loving person whose primary interests were always her husband and children. She was married, like her sister, at the age of eighteen, and was deeply in love with her husband, Peter Pelham. Her warmly affectionate letters to "my own dear" and "my beloved husband" are very appealing. But the marriage brought troubles. Her Quaker church of Philadelphia frowned on the union of a believer with a "hireling minister" and disassociated her. And then, very tragically, Peter died.[12]

Martha Coffin Pelham remarried in 1829, becoming Martha Coffin Wright. Her new and well-loved husband was the lawyer David Wright, who, while not a reformer himself, looked upon his wife's ideas tolerantly, raising no objections to her beliefs or activities. As for Martha, she devoted her major efforts to making a fine home at Auburn, New York, for her husband, and to caring properly for her children. Her voluminous letters were in many ways like those of her sister Lucretia, to whom she wrote frequently. They were packed with comments on her home and on the community, with proper space devoted to such important matters as the making of strawberry jam, the characteristics of the new minister, and the progress of little Willie's colic. They were permeated with a glowing love for her husband, her children, and her friends. As the children grew up and left home, the letters were devoted more and more to the giving of good advice from her vast store of experience. Unfortunately for the student of feminism, however, she seldom commented on women's rights, even though she traveled a good deal and knew many of the leaders intimately. This lack of comment continued even after the children were grown and Mrs. Wright spent relatively more of her time in advancing the movement.

Martha Wright emerges from her letters as a thoroughly kind and good woman of very high and conservative personal moral standards. Early in her second marriage she wrote with obvious shock of attending a rural dance and seeing ladies "sitting in the gentlemen's laps & thinking nothing of being kissed—and the waltzing!"[13] On the other hand, her personal philosophy of the world was liberal and tolerant, and she was at times concerned lest her instructions to her children be nullified by outside influences. Speaking of the presumed importance of a mother's teachings, she commented rather sadly: "I often wonder tho' whether the preaching does any good when the teachings at school conflict so often."[14]

One of Martha Wright's more attractive characteristics was a keen sense of humor, which contrasted pleasantly with the overserious attitude of most feminists, including Mrs. Wright's sister. When Mrs. Wright was confused with Paulina Wright Davis at a convention, she wrote lightly to her husband about the incident, saying that the mixup was all right with her if Mrs. Davis did not object.[15] She delighted in calling Susan B. Anthony "Banthony." When her sister moved to a new home in Philadelphia she wrote a five-verse dirge which began:

> Weep for the glory of 330!
> Weep for James Mott and Lucretia, his mate,
> Weep that the thought ever entered their pate,
> Of selling the mansion of 330!

After the last verse were the words "Boo Hoo."[16]

Like her sister Lucretia, Martha believed in a "rational" religion, but her concepts were much more liberal and tolerant

25

than her sister's. In later years she thus consoled a daughter for the loss of a child: "As to the teachings of the pulpit or the Bible, they come only from fallible mortals like ourselves, & their opinion is worth just as much as yours or mine—neither more nor less—*less* if it seems less rational."[17] She rejected the idea of a jealous and cruel God who punished with eternal fire as contrary to the kindly goodness which she herself felt for mankind and hence attributed to the Deity.

Mrs. Wright's views about women were not extreme, and in general agreed with those of her sister. While she wanted increased rights and opportunities for women, she supported by both precept and practice the idea that the most important functions of women were as wives and mothers. She was a wholehearted supporter of the excellence of her own sex, even as against her beloved husband. When he suggested that women were not very considerate of other women, she flared back with something approaching asperity that men were even less considerate of other members of their own sex. Mrs. Wright was always loyal to her friends. When the feminists split in 1869, Henry Blackwell made a vigorous effort to persuade her to join the seceders, but she remained completely and unquestioningly loyal to her close friend Mrs. Stanton. Altogether, Mrs. Wright was an admirable woman—one of the best-balanced and most attractive of the early feminists.

In striking contrast to the Coffin sisters were the Grimké sisters, Sarah and Angelina. The Coffin girls were New Englanders and natural homemakers, while the Grimkés were Southern-born and natural spinsters, even though one of them ultimately married. The Coffins were imbued with large tinctures of moderation and common sense; the Grimkés were emotional, doctrinaire, and unbending, seeming at times to go out of their way to search for trouble. The Coffins were warmly human and very popular with their fellow workers; the Grimkés were rigid, self-righteous, and uncompromising, provoking outright hostility even among those who agreed in general with their point of view. Mrs. Stanton once burst out in exasperation: "Good Heavens!! what fools those Grimkés are!"[18] Mrs. Mott confessed to Mrs. Stanton that "I have little hope of them."[19] Even the kindly and tolerant Mrs. Wright had something less than her usual warmth when she wrote upon hearing of Sarah's death: "I suppose she liked the sort of life she had, but it doesn't seem like a very delightful one to me."[20]

Sarah and Angelina Grimké were the daughters of a prosperous and conservative Charleston slave-owner, a member of the legislature who moved in the better social circles. There was something over twelve years' difference in their ages, Sarah having been born late in 1792 and Angelina early in 1805. When Sarah was sixteen and Angelina a very little girl, Sarah was "initiated into the circles of dissipation and folly,"[21] which meant no more than that she started to go to balls and to attend the theater. A few years later she devoted her life to the nursing of a sick father, even taking him to Philadelphia to consult the famous Dr. Physic. Her Philadelphia experience was a real eye opener, and after the death of her father in 1819 she was glad to leave an unhappy home life and start to earn her own living by teaching in Philadelphia (1821). She was very much attracted by the Quakers, whom in time she joined.

Meantime Angelina was growing up in Charleston, a kind-hearted, sentimental, emotional young lady. Though she accepted the institution of slavery, she was sympathetic with the slaves, and sometimes at night would slip out of the house to comfort one of them who had been punished severely during the day. The turning point of her life came with a visit to her sister in Philadelphia in 1828. Religion and ethics increasingly dominated her thoughts, and she soon decided that the fashionable life was wicked, whereupon she immediately tore up a Scott novel she had been reading, and stuffed her fancy veils into a pillow. She was converted to the cause of abolition, and the two sisters demonstrated their faith by sitting among the

27

Negroes in the back pews of the church, after which they might return home and sit in solitude, weeping over the evils of slavery.

Angelina soon made her permanent home in Philadelphia, and from this time until their deaths the lives of the two sisters were closely interlaced. Both now were Quakers. Both were apparently confirmed spinsters, for Angelina at twenty-three had shown no serious interest in the opposite sex, while Sarah was thirty-five. Both appeared frail, and not even their best friends ever accused them of being beautiful. Luckily they could wear the Quaker costume, since later, after they had been ejected from the church, visitors noted that they had very poor taste in clothes. Angelina was the younger and less unattractive; also she was in general happier, more buoyant, and more self-reliant than Sarah. She seldom hesitated in making a decision, and almost never later regretted her choice. Sarah was highly introspective and felt less certainty over her decisions; she would ponder a problem at great length, consult with others, and then be uncertain of the validity of her choice. Sarah was also a rather intimidating person, looking more than a little severe and even grim.

Abolition soon dominated the thoughts and lives of the Grimkés. Angelina published in 1830 a book which she called *An Appeal to the Christian Women of the South,* and which had at least the effect of making her an unwelcome visitor in her home town. But writing was not enough, and the sisters offered their services to the American Anti-Slavery Society as speakers. Their first efforts were among the women's auxiliaries near New York City, but while they had adequate voices their presentations were not effective. At this point the eminent Abolitionist and orator Theodore D. Weld took a hand, spending several months in training Angelina. As a result of his efforts Angelina became a very effective speaker. Sarah, on the other hand, remained unimpressive.

The most exciting experience of the sisters was a speaking

tour through New England in the years 1837-38. At first they spoke only to women, but then to both sexes, which was considered daring in spite of the pioneering efforts of Frances Wright a decade earlier. The Congregational ministry was very hostile as the Grimkés spoke to mixed audiences, even in the churches, and said so vigorously, whereupon the Grimkés were increasingly determined to uphold their "rights," and embraced the cause of feminism. Angelina declaimed that "I recognize no rights but human rights . . . for in Jesus Christ there is neither male nor female."[22] Sarah was at least equally positive; replying to an invitation to speak, she said that the answer would be "no" if the audience were entirely women, and "yes" if men were also admitted.[23] Possibly the peak of the whole speaking tour was an appearance of Angelina before a Massachusetts legislative committee, of course composed exclusively of men.

The swing of the Grimkés to feminism produced strong reactions among their male Abolitionist friends. Some of the men, such as Garrison, approved their position; Garrison expressed this attitude a trifle later in the London antislavery convention, and it fitted very well with his efforts to take over control of the American Anti-Slavery Society. But many men, such as Weld and Whittier, pleaded with the Grimkés to soft-pedal feminism. They pointed out that they themselves favored woman's rights and acted upon its principles, but insisted that injecting feminism into the abolition crusade merely made the task of the Abolitionists even more difficult by introducing an extraneous issue and thereby increasing the opposition. The Grimkés shrugged aside this point of view impatiently, with the retort that if women were given greater rights abolition would be attained more quickly.

By this time the Grimkés apparently were confirmed spinsters, for Angelina was thirty-three in 1838, while Sarah celebrated her forty-sixth birthday before the end of the year. Their writings and speeches seemed to label them not only pro-woman but also anti-man. Sarah took the lead in describing the sisters' attitude toward sex in its relation to social problems, publishing in 1838 her little volume *Letters on the Condition of Women and the Equality of the Sexes*. Her starting point was the Bible, which she insisted she should interpret according to her reason, since the accuracy of the translation could not be trusted until women learned Latin and Greek and could do their own translating. In her interpretation, God had made man and woman equal, and their fall from grace brought more blame to Adam than to Eve, because Adam allowed himself to be convinced by another mortal. As Adam's punishment he was filled with a lust for power, which occasioned all the trouble in the world because it operated to oppress peace-loving and docile women. Now the time had come when wives should rise and demand equality with their husbands; the Biblical injunction for wives to subject themselves to their husbands had been a prophecy rather than a command. In fact all women should revolt and attain their full stature. They should stop spending their time and energy on such frivolities as clothes, and coöperate with men of good will in the reformation of the world. As to marriage, Sarah had a very low opinion of it. Marriage for the woman was a fraud, an imposition, a device for spiritual debasement, for "under the gentle appellation of *protection,* that which they have leaned upon has proved a broken reed at best, and oft a spear."[24]

The presumably permanent way of life of the Grimké sisters received a rough jolt in May 1838, when Angelina received in the mail a proposal of marriage from her speaking mentor, Theodore Weld.[25] With many capitals and underlinings indicating his perturbation and the depths of his feeling, he declared modestly that he realized that his declaration would surprise and shock Angelina and that he had no hope his feelings would be reciprocated. Then, apparently worried that it was not entirely fitting that a man who had dedicated his life to God and to abolition should permit his mind to be diverted to more earthly and pleasant affairs, he added for his own justification: "I *do* love the God our righteousness *better* than I love *you.*" These words may in turn have bothered him as seeming to limit his affection for Angelina, for he explained: "And it is *because* I love him *better* that I love you *as* I do."

Angelina replied to this qualified adoration by agreeing that in one way she was surprised, because she had never received any clue as to his feelings, but that in another sense she felt no surprise "because in the depths of my own heart *there was found a response.*" Then followed a cascade of passionate letters, marked most notably by intensive soul-searching on the part of this extravagantly pious pair. Angelina was particularly horrified to discover that her mind wandered from the glories of God and the necessity of reforming the world to longings to be with her beloved. "I laid awake thinking why it was that my heart longed and panted and reached after you as it does. Why my Savior and my God is not enough to *satisfy* me. Am I sinning, am I ungrateful, *am I an* IDOLATOR?"

Theodore and Angelina found an agreement of minds and spirits seldom attained in this imperfect world. They agreed in religious fervor and in reforming zeal. They agreed that husband and wife should have equal voices in all important decisions. They agreed that marriage should be on the highest level, and not marked by the "innumerable, horrible, unspeakable, earthy, sensual and devilish distortions of married life." They even agreed on the unusual proposition that a formal marriage ceremony was not essential, since they were already married in the eyes of God, even if they never saw each other again.

The presumably unnecessary marriage actually took place on May 14, 1838, with one of its results the expulsion of the Grimkés from the Society of Friends. Since the parties disapproved the ordinary ritual, they devised their own. The ceremony took place in a private home before a group of friends which included Negroes to demonstrate their hostility to segregation. First, Theodore spoke of the wickedness of the superiority given to the husband by law, and promised to use no influence upon his wife except love. Then Angelina promised to love and honor, but of course not to obey. Following these statements everyone knelt, and there were prayers by Theodore, by Angelina, by a colored minister, by a white minister, and by Sarah. The marriage certificate was then read aloud by William Lloyd Garrison and signed by all present, after which the company spent the evening in elevating conversation.

Angelina's marriage created certain problems of intellectual readjustment, since both sisters had at various times expressed considerable skepticism about such unions. Angelina insisted that her views about women had not changed, and developed a very ingenious rationalization: "O! how often has my heart mourned over the *misery* of married life, and prayed to be saved from it, and saved from the responsibilities of a family until my Father *had prepared* me to enter upon them in his fear and to *his glory*. I believe He has heard my prayers."

Sarah was confronted with even greater difficulties, since many of her previous remarks about marriage had been exceedingly harsh, but she was equal to the crisis. Her great inspiration was that the Lord had specially planned Angelina's marriage as an aid to all female lecturers: "I believe the Lord has brought her into it that she may vindicate the character of female lecturers."[26] Furthermore, the marriage should aid the cause of women by showing that the same woman who can hold a large audience spellbound can also perform quietly and modestly the duties of a housekeeper and wife. In this connection, added Sarah, Angelina also exhibits another important aspect of ideal female character by "sharing with her husband *in every respect* the headship of the house."[27]

Angelina's marriage may have been designed by God to

32

promote the cause of feminine independence, but its most obvious immediate effects were in the opposite direction. Angelina, like less eminent women, retired to her home, which she found quite demanding, and particularly because Sarah was a permanent part of the new family. Soon she had a baby, and Charles Stuart Weld took a great deal of her time. Combined with her domestic preoccupations was increasingly poor health, including difficulties with her voice, and her public appearances became rare. More significantly, her interest in feminism declined, and she even expressed the heresy of doubting the value of the women's conventions that were such an important part of the current agitation. In fact she held that "woman must have time to grow gradually into the new conditions we have planned for her & which nature, common sense & religion demand."[28]

Sarah, remaining a spinster, was more persistent in her advocacy of feminine rights. She continued to speak and to write on feminism and abolition, although frequently with the effect of intimidating rather than persuading: "She frightens the ministers['] wives about the country half to death, talking on the woman question."[29] Sarah's message was that women were being prepared by suffering for a glorious future: "I see in the debasement and sufferings of woman a process of purification, an ordeal to prepare her for the mission upon which she is now entering."[30] On another occasion she wrote: "My head & my heart bear continually the thought of woman, her condition & her destiny—the one as ignoble as the other is glorious."[31] But what is this mission? "Her holy mission is to bring peace on earth and good-will to man."[32] But Sarah Grimké's ardor, her earnestness, her deeply felt beliefs were not enough. Personally unattractive, she read poorly her dull speeches, which were inaudible to most of her audiences. The effective part of the team had been Angelina, and now Angelina was practically out of the picture. The Grimkés had performed their small function of helping to create the early

33

feminist movement, but their long-run influence on the nature of that movement was negligible.

Traveling with the Grimkés on part of their tour of 1837 was a young New England lady of twenty-seven, who was on the threshold of a distinguished career as Abolitionist and feminist. In some ways Abigail ("Abby") Kelley resembled the Grimkés. She was also a Quaker, had started her adult career as a teacher, and then had dedicated herself to the reform of the world. But the differences were at least as impressive as the similarities. While Miss Kelley had her detractors who heartily disliked her, most people agreed that she was personally attractive to both men and women. Parker Pillsbury, himself a reformer of considerable reputation, proclaimed that "Abby is after all, *The Woman* of the age."[33] Abby Kelley was obviously Irish in heritage, and her Quaker faith came from inheritance rather than from conversion. Her family responsibilities were unusually large because after her father's death she took over the management of the affairs of a rather helpless mother. Convinced of the overwhelming importance of abolition by reading W. L. Garrison, she made the difficult decision to give up her teaching in favor of the arduous and precarious occupation of female abolition orator.

Abolition was the overwhelming passion of Abby Kelley throughout her life, but with the same New England experiences as the Grimkés, she felt the same resentment from the opposition she received as a woman. On more than one occasion she had trouble from her fellow Abolitionists, many of whom objected vigorously even to having her serve on committees; Lewis Tappan at one time announced that he could not work with a woman. Miss Kelley attended the London antislavery convention of 1840, with the same unhappy reaction as Mrs. Mott and Mrs. Stanton. Altogether, her acceptance of feminism is easily understandable.[34]

During the 1840's Abby Kelley spent lavishly of her time and energy in the cause of abolition, particularly on speaking trips through Pennsylvania and New York. Her letters were filled with both the hardships and the pleasures of travel, with descriptions of successful, well-attended, and enthusiastic meetings, and with other accounts of poorly attended and hostile meetings. Now and then she mentioned an egg flying in her direction, and once expressed her relief that the egg contained a chicken and hence did not spot her. She was intensely in earnest, and worked to the limit of her strength, which possibly explains in part why no spark of humor enlivened the accounts of her experiences. She was entirely convinced of the truth and vital importance of her work, even if the recipients of her philanthropic efforts were apathetic: "All great reforms for the bettering of any class of people, have not started among the people to be benefited, but by those who saw their need."[35] Her thoughts were dominated by abolition, with feminism running a poor second, and this relationship continued to exist throughout her career even though she spoke at several woman's rights conventions during the 1850's. "The cause" in her mind was always abolition.

During the early 1840's a new dimension was added to the life of Abby Kelley. She fell in love with Stephen Symonds Foster, a fellow worker for abolition and also a strong believer in women's rights: falling in love with a man of any other beliefs would have been inconceivable. This love affair brought a great outflowing of letters in which Abby revealed many of her inner thoughts and feelings.[36]

Stephen S. Foster may be described without exaggeration as an extraordinary man. Less than two months older than Abby Kelley, he had been born on a farm at Canterbury, New Hampshire. After learning the trade of carpenter, he decided that his real mission was to bring salvation to the Middle West—a task which Lyman Beecher was just then proclaiming as the most vital necessity for the future of America. To prepare himself for this holy mission he entered Dartmouth in 1834, at an age considerably greater than his classmates'. A stormy college career ending prematurely, he tried Union Theological Seminary (1838-39), where he finally decided that the Congregational ministry was not for him. He entered the abolition movement for full-time work in 1839.

The Foster career was never peaceful. As a pacifist Stephen refused to obey a call for militia muster, and then preferred to go to jail rather than to pay his fine. His religious and moral standards diverged widely from those of the college church, and during his abbreviated college career he castigated the church for tolerating slavery and buttressing the subordination of women. Reliable witnesses reported many of his intemperate remarks, including his labeling of the church as "a synagogue of Satan," but although good New Hampshirites resented such remarks they were slow to take action. Not until 1841, several years after he had discarded Dartmouth, was he ejected from the church.[37]

Foster put his views of the church on record in 1843, when he published a little volume entitled *The Brotherhood of Thieves, or A True Picture of the American Church and Clergy*. With scathing and vituperative diatribes, he accused the church of exploring "the deep and fathomless abominations of those *pious* thieves who gain their livelihood by preaching sermons and stealing babies."[38] He said that the existing church supported such horrors as adultery, man-stealing, and piracy because it tolerated slavery. Such views, always expressed extravagantly, ensured Foster of constantly being a storm center. While he had his ardent supporters such as James Russell Lowell, who wrote a poem in his honor, and Abby Kelley, who fell in love with him, he was continually in trouble. His abolition meetings were among the most turbulent of the period.

The love of Abby Kelley for Stephen Foster was no doubt inspired in part by her complete approval of his views. Her own logical, intense, and humorless mind had arrived at the same ideas, but Stephen expressed them in more picturesque and provocative language. In addition, Stephen was none too well, and hence appealed to Abby's strong motherly instincts. Altogether, she threw the whole passion of her intensely emotional nature into her affection for Stephen, and her yearnings ran through a long series of letters to her betrothed.[39] She reiterated frequently her "always ardent" feelings, and insisted that her loved one was constantly in her thoughts: "I have thought of you every cold night—aye and every warm one too." She asserted her domesticity by insisting that "I am a devout worshipper of the house-hold [sic] God." She signed her letters with some such ending as "Good night—Angels guard your slumbers—Your Abby."

Abby Kelley's feelings toward Stephen were vastly complicated by her lifelong devotion to abolition, or, as she called it, "the cause." Having dedicated her life to the crusade for Negro rights, her conscience gave her severe twinges when she thought of retiring from lecturing to become a housewife. When Stephen from time to time urged an early marriage she greeted the idea with ardor, but then counseled delay because of her moral commitments. At one time she toyed with the idea of delaying any meeting with her beloved lest she could not control her affections.

Stephen's letters were also affectionate, but the reader does not feel the emotional intensity expressed by Abby. On one occasion he argued for early marriage by saying: "I am heart sick of bricks & flatirons for winter companions." Such a sentiment was understandable, but it hardly conveyed the implications of the sort of wild passion that a woman of Abby's temperament might have preferred.

Abby and Stephen finally were married on December 31, 1845, with Abby doubting that their friends would find sufficient spare time to attend the ceremony. After the marriage Abby stayed at home, and this way of life became particularly necessary after the birth of a daughter, Alla. She was an efficient homemaker and a devoted mother, her interests centering around her baby daughter. Apparently she treated Stephen somewhat like a second child, pampering what she considered his delicate constitution. As a feminist she believed that husband and wife should be equal, and she emphasized the point to Stephen by a scathing description of a neighboring wife who she felt was no more than a slave. But she went a good deal farther than this. She had warned Stephen before their marriage that she had a managing disposition and that she would make him toe the mark. This she did.

The clear dominance of the wife in this particular marriage, together with Abby's greater reputation in the world of reform, brought certain psychological problems to Stephen. Ultimately he solved them to his own satisfaction, writing to his wife: "Your great success, however, throws me entirely in the shade, and might awaken my envy if it were not, after all, *my own*. As it is, I can only congratulate myself on the exercise of that good sense & sound discrimination which made you my *first* choice among all the women of my acquaintance, & the good fortune which placed such a *prize* within my grasp." Possibly Stephen, in spite of his bold public statements, really liked to be dominated.

As Alla grew a little older, her mother felt that she could be left with others, and that "the cause" could again be promoted actively. Sometimes her mother stayed home while her father traveled, sometimes the situation was reversed, and sometimes Alla was left with a third party despite certain neighborhood criticisms. Mrs. Foster continued to insist on the primacy of abolition even though at certain times she could not be active in its support. As she put the situation: "The person at home holds the key to our heart's dearest interests, because there the affections cluster. I say of our hearts' interests—Let me not be misunderstood. I trust that both of us are willing to lay home, friends, all on the altar of the great principles which lie at the foundation of the world's renovation."

Mrs. Foster argued with herself continually about the relative importance of home and of abolition, but consoled herself with the conviction that her marriage was happy and that the meetings of both herself and her husband were better than before the marriage. While she regretted she had not married sooner, she also worried as to whether she was putting her husband too high in her affections, so that he even obscured God. One is reminded of Theodore Weld, and the comparison is intensified by the similarity of her solution: "My thoughts are *too much* with thee—I fear I love the creation more than the creator; but in analyzing my feelings, I believe it is only the *image* of the creator which I love in the creature."

The greatest single problem was of course Alla, who was the very center of Abby's emotional life. When Alla was sick, no other thought could compete; in one case Abby went to New York to consult a clairvoyant as to proper treatment. As an only child born relatively late in her parents' life, Alla was well nurtured and well educated—surrounded by love. And yet she never seemed to mature satisfactorily. While at college she wrote rather pathetically: "The children of good and great parents are apt to [be] ugly or forceless, and I think you and I should be thankful that I am not any worse." After Vassar, Alla became a teacher. She never married.

Abby Kelley Foster's outside activities declined not only because of her overwhelming interest in Alla but because of ill-health, her menopause probably being a factor. After 1860 she practically stopped lecturing because of difficulty with her voice. Her greatest later publicity came in 1874, when she refused to pay taxes to a government which she had no part in electing. Other feminists were indignant when her property was sold for taxes: "Because it had the power, the city sold her home over her head, and took so much money as it pleased, just as any other robber might have done, and with no better right."[40] William Lloyd Garrison and James Freeman Clarke were among those who wrote letters of praise for the Foster action. Actually, however, the outcome was far short of spectacular. The farm was sold to cover taxes of $82.84, being bought for $100 by a neighbor who immediately sold it back to the Fosters. Possibly a principle had been supported, but in fact the taxes were merely paid indirectly rather than directly, and the only real effect was a small flurry of publicity.

Abby Kelley Foster was among the many women who were drawn from abolition into women's rights. Her contribution to feminism was extremely moderate in terms of either ideas or organization or propaganda. But she did illustrate quite well the way in which a significant group of women were converted to feminism. In a very real sense, American feminism was a by-product of the abolition movement.

3

Elizabeth Cady Stanton

ELIZABETH CADY STANTON was the most prominent and influential of the pioneer American feminists. Not that she originated the movement, even though she spoke at times as though she had, and not that she created a distinctive philosophy, for in fact she was never a philosopher, but because she was the dynamo of feminism, the centrifugal force that held the movement together, and the most effective propagandist in the drive to expand the opportunities of women. While an exact weighing of her specific contributions cannot be made, and while any major changes result from the contributions of thousands of often unidentifiable people, at the end of a long life Mrs. Stanton could quite properly view with great satisfaction the realization of many of her dreams, and the near accomplishment of many others, including national woman suffrage under a constitutional amendment.

Any written description of Elizabeth Stanton almost inevitably fails to convey a proper impression of her real personal attractiveness. Built much like a fire hydrant and not over five feet, three inches tall, she was plump as a girl and even plumper as a mature woman. Her features were dominated by a broad, flat nose which eliminated any possible claim to classic beauty. Most striking were her sparkling blue eyes, which seemed always filled with pleasure and innocent wonder, and which retained their impression of youthful joy in life even when she became a very old woman. Her hair turned gray while she was still young, and for most of her public career appeared in gorgeous white ringlets. She dressed carefully and simply, a wise course in view of her bulk. For plat-

41

form appearances she favored black, with white trimmings at neck and wrists.

Elizabeth Stanton gave an impression of approachability and of dignity at one and the same time. Her slightly homely features made her appear kindly, benevolent, generous, wise, and motherly. Dozens of young women were inspired to bring her their personal problems, which she took the necessary time to hear about in detail before offering her wise counsel. At the same time she always retained a real dignity, with something of reserve. Even her close friends such as Susan Anthony and Martha Wright almost always addressed her as Mrs. Stanton, while Miss Anthony, only five years younger, was ordinarily called Susan. The only friend who regularly called her Elizabeth was the considerably older Mrs. Mott.

Physically, Mrs. Stanton was extraordinarily healthy and vigorous, with very few periods of ill-health. Even childbirth seemed relatively easy, except for her last child, a 12¼-pound boy, about whom she wrote: "I never suffered so much. I was sick all the time before he was born, and I have been weak ever since."[1] Possibly her age, which was forty-four, made a difference. But this episode was exceptional. Caring for a husband and seven children might well have been a good excuse for frequent exhaustion, but actually Mrs. Stanton had surplus energy to entertain frequently and on a large scale, to visit and to receive many visitors, to write copiously to her friends and for publication, and to undertake extensive speaking tours. These lecture trips were a particular drain with their difficult traveling, including night trips by horse and buggy, their bad food, their dirty beds, and their greeting of a continual flood of people. At the very time when Susan Anthony seemed tired and drawn, Mrs. Stanton would appear fresh, vigorous, and blooming. Even after she passed eighty, and was in fact slowing down perceptibly, she continued to give the impression of dynamic vigor.

Intellectually and emotionally, Mrs. Stanton was well

42

equipped for her work. An even and buoyant temperament gave always the impression of gayety and love of life. A superior intelligence seized the essential points of an argument and developed them clearly and incisively. Add to these advantages an effective use of words and figures of speech, an attractive personal appearance, a voice which remained beautiful through almost her entire life, and a personal magnetism coming from good health, and her effectiveness as a speaker is easily understandable. But Mrs. Stanton was much more than an effective speaker. Her breadth of thought, physical tirelessness, extroverted nature, relative immunity to criticism, great personal dignity, and obvious efficiency made her an ideal executive and the head of almost every organization in which she participated. From time to time she offered to step aside in favor of someone more effective, if such a person could be found, but none ever was. She seldom became upset and peevish from criticism, even when it was particularly personal and nasty; in fact she saved such diatribes and later published many of them in her history of woman suffrage. She didn't sulk and mope over disappointments, and her handling of her co-workers was a pleasure to observe. Involved in these various traits was an ability to inspire intense personal devotion. No greater tribute could be paid than that of Susan Anthony, who after a generation of work with Mrs. Stanton could speak sincerely of her as "our glorious Chief."[2]

Mrs. Stanton could and did like people with whom she disagreed, and had a larger sense of humor than many of her colleagues; she had no hesitation about telling humorous stories in which she was the butt of the joke. A nice case was that of her nephew, Robert Stanton, of whom she was very fond in spite of his anti-feminism. Her reaction after reading an article he had written: "Bless me! what hardships these dear men have endured to make flowery paths of ease for us women! and then it makes me blush to think how we berate them in our suffrage conventions. I think we should pass some eulogistic resolutions at our next convention, as to the beauty of their muscular system, their courage, their patience under suffering, their self sacrifice in making this rugged earth a paradise for the weaker sex!"[3]

Mrs. Stanton's virtues were impressive, but luckily for the self-respect of more ordinary mortals, they were accompanied by flaws. Her vigorous self-confidence was at times difficult to distinguish from blatant egotism; possibly of significance was her handwriting, which as she grew older became continually larger and blacker and more difficult to read. Her broadly conceived and often doctrinaire ideas sometimes passed the limits of plausibility, and often involved logical contradictions. Her reaction against the traditional brought interest in such oddities as dress reform, spiritualism, theosophy, and phrenology.

Mrs. Stanton's choice in friends was at times a trifle undiscriminating, and even distressed her associates. The eccentric George Francis Train traveled with the Stanton party through Kansas in 1867, and upon the group's return provided the funds for a periodical, *Revolution,* which was devoted not only to feminism but also to the somewhat questionable Train financial schemes. Most of Mrs. Stanton's friends considered Train as more than a little cracked, and he was a definite factor in the split of the feminists in 1869. The best Mrs. Stanton could say for him was that he was effective advertising. Mrs. Annie Besant was another friend; Mrs. Stanton was apparently quite fascinated both by the woman and by her theosophy, a distillation of various occult beliefs from the Far East. Still other friends were Theodore and Elizabeth Tilton, who ultimately became involved in the juiciest and most scandalous of court cases, as Theodore sued his pastor Henry Ward Beecher, America's most popular minister, for misconduct with his wife. Theodore Tilton was for a time president of the National Woman Suffrage Association, and when he sued Beecher he wrote to ask Mrs. Stanton whether she would testify on his behalf; luckily the need did not arise. Most difficult of all was Mrs. Stanton's vigorous support of the notorious Victoria Woodhull, whose marital theories and practices were a crying scandal. Only with great effort was Mrs. Stanton pulled out of this embarrassing situation.[4] Such cases produced obvious recriminations and problems.

The fact that Mrs. Stanton was outgoing and friendly does not imply that her life was uncomplicated, or that she was not beset by the psychological stresses and strains so familiar to other human beings. Quite the contrary. Severe emotional experiences early in life left an ineradicable impression. While she moved from abolition to feminism like so many of her colleagues, her feminism can by no means be credited to her experiences as an Abolitionist. Feminism to her was a direct and almost inescapable consequence of the experiences of her early life.

Elizabeth Cady Stanton, born Elizabeth Cady, was the daughter of the conservative and prosperous lawyer Daniel Cady, whose favorable reputation in the community enabled him to have a modest political career. Elizabeth naturally had the physical advantages of a well-to-do home, and the intellectual benefit of a good education. She was plump, active, and fun-loving, a bit adventurous, and something of a tomboy, as she participated enthusiastically in sports and games with what was then considered a masculine drive to win. She was somewhat more active and mischievous than the usual child, and later remembered being punished frequently for "tantrums," which might have been violent displays of temper, but probably were only vigorous childhood pranks. Concerning her badly received actions she wrote much later: "I suppose they were really justifiable acts of rebellion against the tyranny of those in authority,"[5] but probably this statement represented more a frame of mind than a fair interpretation of the facts.

The really decisive influence in the life of Elizabeth was her relations with her father, as she made crystal-clear in her autobiography. Judge Cady was proud of his name and desirous of perpetuating it. Unfortunately for his dream he had but one boy among his six children, and while he loved his daughters he realized that the name Cady would be lost whether or not they married. In these circumstances the son was the center of his father's affections. When Elizabeth was eleven, her brother graduated from Union College. But he returned home a sick young man and took to his bed. His father sat at his bedside hour after hour, but he grew worse and worse, and ultimately died.[6]

As the Judge kept vigil beside the casket of his dead son, his thoughts must have been tragic. While he sat tense and dry-eyed, mourning the end of his high hopes, Elizabeth stole into the room and crept into his arms, which tightened convulsively. In a shaken voice he breathed: "Oh, my daughter, I wish you were a boy!" Touched deeply, Elizabeth threw her arms around her father's neck and whispered: "I will try to be all my brother was."[7]

From this incident Elizabeth acquired a horror of deaths and funerals, and possibly some misgivings about religion and the church. More important for her future, however, was her resolution to replace her brother in her father's life. She devoted her major efforts to such male occupations as caring for a horse and studying Greek and mathematics; a vague hope existed that she might go to Union College, as had her brother. Her dearest aspiration was that some day her father would say that a girl was as good as a boy. But he never did. On one occasion she received prizes in Greek and mathematics and immediately rushed home to tell her father the good news. He was pleased, but also sad, murmuring with a sigh: "Oh, you should have been a boy." Whereupon Elizabeth broke down and cried.

As Elizabeth grew older the idea persisted that if she could only achieve in the same ways as a boy she would please her father. She apparently never realized that her assumption was utterly unrealistic, since a conservative father would feel only shocked and critical concerning a daughter who tried to be a son. As late as 1855, when Mrs. Stanton was forty years old and a well-established matron, she wrote to Susan Anthony: "I passed through a terrible scourging when last at my father's. I cannot tell you how deep the iron entered my soul. I never felt more keenly the degradation of my sex. To think that all in me of which my father would have felt a proper pride had I been a man, is deeply mortifying to him because I am a woman."[8]

Elizabeth Stanton's inner turmoil and frustration did not prevent her from enjoying life at Emma Willard's school at Troy, which, though not Union, was an excellent institution; her one criticism was that it did not take boys. Then she returned home to enjoy the normal pleasures of a young woman filling the idle years between school and marriage. She delighted particularly in arguing with the law students who were being trained by her father, and felt a particular thrill when she could get the better of one of them in an argument. Every year she visited her relative Gerrit Smith, the reformer, and at his home was immersed in the reforming spirit; quite naturally she accepted ideals of reform, and particularly abolition, even though her father was not enthusiastic about reformers, including Smith.

While visiting Gerrit Smith, Elizabeth met a certain Henry Stanton, who, although ten years older than she, was extremely active as an abolition speaker of considerable promise. In time he asked her to marry him, and she accepted, with of course the proviso that there be no "obey" in the marriage ceremony. At the moment she was rebounding from an unhappy love affair with her sister's husband, and her real reason for marriage may well have involved both a sense of guilt and an unrecognized revolt from her father, for the Judge felt a great lack of enthusiasm for an Abolitionist as a son-in-law. Henry would take her away from her childhood home with its close associa-

47

tions with her father, and in fact he promised her a glamorous wedding trip to Europe.

Henry always had a deep affection for Elizabeth. Whenever he was forced to leave home he dreamed of her at night and wrote love letters during the day; when she left him he worried continually about her safety. The emotions of Elizabeth are more difficult to analyze. Her autobiographical comment on the marriage is more than a trifle noncommittal, being merely that it was "without more than the usual matrimonial friction."[9] Her letters were not particularly affectionate, but the evidence is incomplete, since she destroyed most of her correspondence. Upon one occasion she insisted that letters be directed to her and not to her husband because, as she said: "I am as well known here as he is."[10] At another time she wrote to a correspondent objecting to having letters addressed to E. C. Stanton. She declared specifically that she did not much care whether the "Mrs." was used, but insisted emphatically that the E. C. should appear as E. Cady;[11] the father influence obviously was still strong. Even more suggestive is the fact that she did not name her first son for her husband, but Daniel Cady for her father; unfortunately this son turned out to be her least admirable child. Her second son was named for Gerrit Smith.

The wedding trip to England was even more exciting than the bride had anticipated. Not only did she witness the fight over the seating of the women delegates at the antislavery convention of 1840, but she met and fell in love with Lucretia Mott.[12] When the Stantons returned to America, Henry studied law with Judge Cady for a year, during which the young couple lived in the Judge's home, after which Henry established a law practice in Boston (1842). Elizabeth's superabundant energy carried her to lectures, church, theaters, and concerts; she even visited Brook Farm for two days. In Boston she met many Abolitionists, such as William Lloyd Garrison, Paulina Wright Davis, Lydia Maria Child, and Maria Chap-

48

man, of whom some would later work with her for women's rights. She also found time to visit Albany, where her father was a member of the legislature, and where she saw efforts to pass a married woman's property act that was favored by no less a person than Governor William H. Seward.

The Boston experience was relatively short because Henry's health was not good, and so in 1847 the Stantons moved to Seneca Falls with their three small sons. Seneca Falls was a sleepy little country town, and while Elizabeth read Emerson's *Essays,* talked Transcendentalism, and insisted that she loved a small town, she still felt a sense of frustration. The thrill of her first years of housekeeping had passed, and she missed the varied activities of the city. True, she had a husband and a growing family, which in time numbered seven sturdy children who all attained maturity, but they did not occupy her mind completely or exhaust her body. Even social activities failed to take up the slack. More and more her thoughts were occupied with the inferior position of women and the talks she had had with Mrs. Mott. Eventually she decided that she could herself promote the interests of women, even in Seneca Falls, if she held a convention to advertise feminine wrongs. Once having made the decision, her first action was to persuade her dear friend Mrs. Mott to join in the venture.

The convention which finally assembled at Seneca Falls in July 1848 has long been credited as the real start of American feminist agitation. The little town was agog, not only because of the subject of the meeting but also because of the attendance of such notables as the well-known Negro reformer Frederick Douglass and Mr. and Mrs. Mott. The most startling action of the convention was the acceptance of a paraphrase of the Declaration of Independence, with the male sex replacing George III and oppressed women replacing the colonists. The idea was the brain child of Mrs. Stanton, and reputedly she and her friends found considerable difficulty in discovering sufficient women's wrongs to make a respectable showing.

Also adopted was a series of resolutions aimed generally at the proposition that "woman is man's equal." Sixty-eight women and thirty-two men signed the final resolutions.

This first convention was followed by others, including a large national assembly each year and smaller regional meetings at other times. Only once before the Civil War was the annual convention omitted; Miss Anthony explained that "there was no convention on account—well, all the women had, or were about to have, children—& Mrs. Rose was ill."[13]

Mrs. Stanton was connected during the 1850's with one of the most advertised and least happy of the manifestations of feminism—an abortive effort to introduce a bloomer costume of full Turkish trousers gathered at the ankles, with an over-skirt coming just below the knees. The purpose of the innova-tion was to free women physically so that the progress of feminine emancipation would be hastened. The center of the agitation was Seneca Falls, Mrs. Stanton and two of her friends being particularly important.

The originator of the costume was Mrs. Elizabeth Smith Miller, a daughter of Gerrit Smith and therefore a relative of Mrs. Stanton. As a schoolgirl Elizabeth wrote to her father that "ladies have enough to attend to without 'holding forth' to larger assemblies than those collected in their own parlors and by their own firesides,"[14] but later in life she changed her mind. Her early life was steeped in the most pious of influences; her mother's letters emphasized the dangers of allowing the dis-tractions of the world to wean her away from Jesus. Apparently she was attracted to her future husband, Charles Miller, mainly because he used neither wine nor tobacco, and wrote rather self-consciously: "Your love for me is greater than mine for you, but I trust mine will increase, & even its present measure is sufficient, I think, to add to your happiness."[15] She hoped that she would be a cheerful and good wife, and expressed her will-ingness to live wherever he desired, but insisted that she would never abandon her own church for his. Above all, she expressed again and again her deep feeling that the love of God was more important than human love. These views apparently did not work well in marriage. Soon Mother Smith was suggesting that her daughter's health might improve if she did less work and took fewer baths; in fact Mother suggested that the regular bath be replaced by a brushing, followed with a two-minute air bath.[16] A little later Father Smith advised daughter Lizzie that a marriage could succeed only if both parties practiced forbearance.

Here was the woman who first adopted the bloomer costume as a means of coping with the mud of west central New York, and probably with no idea of furthering the cause of women's independence. The truth was that her father was a more ardent feminist than she. He was particularly impressed with the implications of the new costume, and insisted that Lizzie continue to wear the bloomers after she had lost her interest.

The woman who gave her name to the new garment was Mrs. Amelia Bloomer, a resident of Seneca Falls. Amelia Bloomer was a small and dainty woman of five feet, four inches, weighing only 100 pounds when she was married. Her dark blue eyes and auburn hair sound attractive, but actually did not inspire anyone to call her beautiful. She insisted that her outstanding trait was modesty, but a phrenological reading now in the possession of the Seneca Falls Historical Society may well have been more accurate when it described her as intelligent, intense, and fond of people, but as a person whose head ruled her heart. It also called her extremely egotistical and ambitious—not for money but for fame. The last sentence of the report has been scratched out, and one cannot help wondering whether Mrs. Bloomer herself deleted it as too critical.

Amelia Bloomer, who was born in New York State, in spite of a meager education taught for a time and then acted as a governess. In 1840 she married the Quaker Dexter C. Bloomer and moved to Seneca Falls, where her husband edited a newspaper, became postmaster, and took up the profession

51

of law. Mrs. Bloomer had great physical vigor and no children, and so tried various occupations, including that of assistant postmaster. Ultimately the most important of her jobs was the editing of a little temperance paper called the *Lily,* which had been sponsored by the local ladies' temperance society, and which started publication in 1849. Mrs. Bloomer may be blamed for the poor quality of the paper, but at least she had no responsibility for the name, to which she always objected.

When Mrs. Miller appeared in Seneca Falls wearing her unusual clothes, Mrs. Bloomer and her husband were in the process of tossing back and forth in their respective papers the idea of a Turkish costume for women. Mrs. Bloomer at first felt dubious about the Miller appearance, but published an account of it, and discovered to her pleased surprise that the circulation of the paper increased and that something of a fad had been created. From 1851 she herself wore the costume, and found herself in great demand as a lecturer. When she accompanied her husband to Mount Vernon, Ohio, she took the *Lily* along, but when the Bloomers moved still further west to Council Bluffs, she abandoned editing. At Council Bluffs the Bloomers became more prosperous and more domestic, adopting two children; in time Dexter became mayor. The bloomer costume was a handicap to Mrs. Bloomer in her new life, but she continued to wear it until approximately the end of the decade.

The influence of Elizabeth Stanton on Mrs. Bloomer and the *Lily* was very striking. When Mrs. Bloomer originated the *Lily* she was not a feminist and the paper was devoted entirely to temperance, but conditions began to change rapidly after the first Stanton article in the fall of 1849. Very soon the *Lily* was dedicated as much to women's rights as to temperance. Mrs. Bloomer began to parrot Mrs. Stanton's views, with the only obvious difference that Mrs. Bloomer gave greater importance to the effects of liquor. For example, Mrs. Bloomer expressed Mrs. Stanton's misgivings about marriage and the laudation of the mother as compared with the father, but then added that even with fine, pious mothers the children might not turn out well because they would "inherit the vices of their drunken, tobacco chewing fathers."[17] Mrs. Bloomer's mimicry did not impress the level-headed Mrs. Stanton, who was never enthusiastic about her colleague, holding her to be a late convert attracted more by the chance of personal publicity than by basic beliefs.[18]

Mrs. Stanton had long toyed with the idea of a reformed costume which would increase women's physical mobility, and greeted the Miller innovation with enthusiasm. Not only would the less hampering clothes permit women to enter more of the male occupations, but also they would decrease the emphasis on feminine sexual characteristics, and in consequence "we shall all lead far purer and higher lives."[19] Henry smiled tolerantly, but must have shocked Elizabeth when he speculated that men would be delighted to learn whether their lady friends had plump or scrawny legs.[20] Father Cady was outraged, and ordered his daughter never to appear in his home clad in this fashion, whereupon Elizabeth flounced back to her own home and cut off all her skirts.

Mrs. Stanton found the reformed dress a physical comfort, but soon experienced other and less happy results. While she was never overconcerned with her personal appearance, she could hardly have failed to realize that her dumpy figure was not improved by the baggy pants and short skirt—and particularly when she added a large, floppy hat. When she walked abroad in the outfit, necks were craned, men whistled, and small boys followed her around. Other feminists had similar experiences, including refusal by their friends to appear on the streets with them. Mrs. Stanton's small son pleaded with his mother to wear a long dress when she visited him. Even more distressing, however, the reformed costume overshadowed more important matters. An audience kept its attention on a speaker's clothes rather than on her message. Conservatives felt themselves justified in their contention that women were trying to ape men—although just how anyone could think that a woman in bloomers looked like a man is difficult to understand.

Mrs. Stanton's first reaction to widespread opposition was a combination of resentment and stubbornness: "Had I counted the cost of the short dress, I would never have put it on; on, however, I'll never take it off, for now it involves a principle of freedom."[21] But her common sense and realism soon prevailed. When Miss Anthony broke down in tears from her experiences, Mrs. Stanton urged her to lengthen her dresses, and Mrs. Stanton herself quietly and unobtrusively took the same action. Within half a dozen years the brief fad was practically dead, and Mrs. Stanton had to record a failure in her record. The experience was useful, however, in showing the undesirability of entering crusades that were only peripheral to the main issue.

During the Civil War Mrs. Stanton and other feminists generally laid aside women's rights propaganda and worked in the Woman's National Loyal League, which had been organized by Mrs. Stanton and Miss Anthony; after all, most of them had been Abolitionists before they had become feminists. At the end of the war they developed an American Equal Rights Association, with Mrs. Mott as president and Mrs. Stanton as vice-president. The hope was to link women with the Negro and to obtain rights for both. Unfortunately for this aspiration, the male reformers, such as William. Lloyd Garrison, Gerrit Smith, and Frederick Douglass, while friendly to women's rights, felt that this was the day of the Negro, and that any efforts to inject the woman question at this time would only hurt the Negro. Mrs. Stanton was highly incensed at this decision and her group withdrew to form the National Woman Suffrage Association, and a second secession produced the American Woman Suffrage Association.

Mrs. Stanton's work during the post-war period centered

largely around the NWSA, although the first two presidents were actually Mrs. Mott and Theodore Tilton. In addition, however, part of her time went to other women's organizations and to a great many lyceum lectures, from which she used the proceeds to send her children to college. When the two suffrage groups were reunited in 1890 as the National American Woman Suffrage Association, Mrs. Stanton was the obvious choice for president.

The views of Elizabeth Stanton came clearly and directly from her own experiences, although not in the sense that she was reacting against personal mistreatment and abuse, for from the casual viewpoint her early life had been happy and her married life had exhibited no outward distress. But her relationship with her father had brought resentment at the inferior position of a girl, and this feeling dominated all her reasoning. Above all, she was the champion of women as against men, although she was more pro-woman than anti-man. She felt no antagonism toward individual men, and objected to men only in the general sense that they tyrannized over women. Interminably she deplored the degradation of women under the cruel laws and vicious customs which had so long kept women in slavery: "Wherever we turn, the history of woman is sad, drear and dark, without any alleviating circumstances."[22] This type of broad, doctrinaire, and extreme statement was typical of Mrs. Stanton and certainly had no relation to her personal experiences.

Mrs. Stanton tended to identify herself with other women in their accomplishments. She reacted this way to a speech by Anna Dickinson: "Whatever any woman does well, I feel that I have done it."[23] Another time she wrote to Whittier: "How proud I am when I see one of my sex doing anything well."[24] Sometimes her pride outran her judgment; for example, the last statement was inspired by the poetry of Felicia Hemans.

The most ecstatic laudation of women came with the birth of Mrs. Stanton's first girl baby: "I am at length the happy mother of a daughter. Rejoice with me all Womanhood, for lo! a champion of the cause is born. I have dedicated her to this work from the beginning. I never felt such sacredness in carrying a child as I have this one, feeling all the time strongly impressed with the belief that I was cherishing the embryo of a mighty female martyr—Glorious hope! May she wear the crown of Martyrdom bravely and patiently, and leave her impress on the world for goodness and truth."[25] Even nature coöperated in the great event, for Elizabeth's labor was short and easy; she sat up immediately after the birth, and within three days was doing her regular housework. The girl did of course become a feminist, but happily she was spared the experience of martyrdom.

Equality of the sexes was not one of the beliefs of Mrs. Stanton. "We are, as a sex," said she, "infinitely superior to men."[26] Whereas the average man is tough, crude, aggressive, and nomadic, the woman is gentle, helpful, home-loving, refined, and pure—"the protector of national virtue; the rightful lawgiver in all our most sacred relations."[27] Women are superior in morals, as witness the trickery of male lawyers and merchants. The bad moral state of the world is to be credited to the suppression of women. "The dogged, unreasonable persecutions of [the] sex in all ages, the evident determination to eliminate, as far as possible, the feminine element in humanity, has been the most fruitful cause of the moral chaos the race has suffered."[28]

Physically and mentally, said Mrs. Stanton, men are now superior, but this superiority is not innate, being based only on the suppression of the opposite sex. Physically, women will in time be able to compete equally if they adopt proper clothes and exercise. Mentally, the feminine mind will equal the masculine mind if given equivalent training; there is no truth in the assertion that men are governed by intellect and women by emotion. Moreover, women have one vital bit of experience that makes them superior to men, and which men can never achieve, and that is motherhood. "This function gives women such wisdom and power as no male ever can possess."[29]

The elevation of women to their proper status and influence in the world depends above all on their proper education so that they can earn their own livings. "When women can support themselves, have their entry to all the trades and professions, with a house of their own over their heads and a bank account, they will own their bodies and be dictators in the social realm."[30] Mrs. Stanton urged her own daughter to obtain suitable professional training, so that she could have money of her own "and not be obliged to depend on any man for every breath you draw."[31]

The proper training of women should of course start in the home; Mrs. Stanton had almost unending quantities of ideas on the training of children. Mother and father should have equality in the home, and children should never receive physical chastisement but be ruled entirely by moral suasion; unfortunately, such suasion did not always work satisfactorily, and she was known to have resorted to bribery. Boys and girls should be treated in the same way. They should wear similar clothes and be given similar training, which meant not only that girls should be taught occupations usually reserved for boys, but that boys should be taught to cook and sew, so that they could at least mend their own clothes and replace lost buttons. This equality between the sexes which was to exist in the home should continue later in life; for example, Mrs. Stanton felt that when a boy and girl went together to any social activity, the girl should pay her fair share of the cost. With this sort of training, which of course included equality of formal education, girls would become at least as capable as boys, both in physique and mentality.

While having infinite confidence in the native capacity of women, Mrs. Stanton could not close her eyes to the obvious fact that many women were silly and frivolous, and that the majority seemed to wear their chains with pleasure. She deplored this complacency, holding that no improvement was possible until women had more respect for themselves, realized their wrongs, and sought to correct them. Only then would women exercise their proper ennobling influence. "One ceases to wonder at the low tastes, animal excesses and physical deformity of our men, in reflecting on the mental vacuity and hopeless folly of our women."[32] In this particular article Mrs. Stanton was bemoaning the follies of mothers, particularly their use of tight bindings on their babies.

The most basic relationship between men and women was in marriage, and "this whole question of woman's rights turns on the pivot of the marriage relation."[33] Particularly was this true because marriage was almost the entire lives of so many women. Mrs. Stanton's opinion of existing marriage was far from favorable, and time after time she derided it as a male institution "rooted in selfishness & sensuality."[34] She asserted rather bitterly that "woman's degradation is in man's idea of his sexual rights,"[35] holding that the legal subserviency of woman—and she accepted Blackstone flatly and without reservation—was designed by men so that they could have complete sexual freedom. The man was protected by law in his insistence upon the satisfaction of his greater physical passions, which meant that the woman had the final ignominy of not being able even to control her own body. Here were the roots of such diverse phenomena as infanticide, prostitution, divorce, and celibacy, with most marriages "a long, hard struggle to make the best of a bad bargain."[36]

Mrs. Stanton expatiated at great length on her solutions of the problem of marriage. In early years she asserted that "I ask for no laws on marriage,"[37] which sounded a trifle as though she wanted to eliminate the marriage institution, but her later writings presented no such desire. Most interesting of her proposals was state action to stop young people from marrying before a certain age (at first eighteen and then twenty-one) so that they would use better judgment, and to fine every woman who conceived a child by a drunken husband.

With marriage, husband and wife were to be equal, which meant first of all the giving of married women rights over their property and children. Above all, however, the wife should have control over her own body. She should have a real choice as to the physical act of sex and as to the bearing of children, which in turn meant a knowledge of how to prevent conception. On one occasion Mrs. Stanton wrote about a woman doctor: "I never saw her, but she made it a specialty to teach women how to avoid a too general perpetuation of the race, which I consider a commendable kind of knowledge to hand down to our overburdened mothers."[38]

Mrs. Stanton throughout her life favored easy divorce; one of her two last published articles, written in the final year of her life, was devoted to the subject.[39] She was thoroughly convinced that unhappy marriages were productive of only trouble and immorality, which could well be disastrous to society. Easy divorce was the correct answer, and the states with lenient laws were for women what Canada had been for the slave.[40]

Mrs. Stanton's obsession with the sufferings of women in marriage naturally raises the question of the extent to which she was reflecting personal experiences. One almost inevitably doubts her own explanation that her ideas were the reaction to an unhappy marriage experience of a friend; but, on the other hand, it is impossible to think of Henry as a cruel and over-demanding, or even thoughtless, husband. When one considers the circumstances of her marriage, the possible partial identification of her husband with her father, the apparent lack of passionately emotional attachment, and her seven children, one senses various possibilities. Certainly Mrs. Stanton was somewhat bored with household chores after she moved to Seneca Falls, and regretted the limiting effects of her domestic activities. "How much I do long to be free from housekeeping and children, so as to have some time to read, and think, and write. But it may be well for me to understand all the trials of woman's lot, that I may more eloquently proclaim them when the time comes."[41] Other evidence pointing in a similar direction is her approval of birth control and her attitude toward her children. While she was an efficient wife and a loving mother and spent her energies freely in advancing the interests of her children, she apparently was happy to leave them with others, as with Susan Anthony, while she went on speaking tours.

Mrs. Stanton's unconventional ideas about marriage were matched by equally unconventional views about religion. In explaining the origin of her thinking she placed considerable emphasis on revival services she attended as a girl.[42] She says she was so deeply impressed that her mind tottered and her health suffered until she adopted a satisfying, "rational" approach to religion. Originally a Presbyterian, she withdrew from the church and showed little interest in religion, thereby differing sharply from most of her co-workers, who were deeply religious. Late in life she wrote down her basic creed, asserting a belief in a beneficent God, in natural law, and in the immortality of the human soul. She refused to accept a special providence, holding that everything followed the natural laws of cause and effect, and felt that the Bible had no special inspiration.[43] The Bible, with its injunctions for the submission of women, was a sore point with Mrs. Stanton, as with other feminists. She felt that the words of St. Paul were only his private opinion, and had been used improperly by men to protect them in their tyranny. Late in life she completed a long-considered project by publishing *The Woman's Bible,* which sought to explain the passages that limited women.

The large, generalized beliefs of Mrs. Stanton involved little respect for usual religion and the Bible, and none for the organized church. She felt that every religion had been hard on women by buttressing men's tyrannical power,[44] and that the American church was as bad as any: "I say the American church is the bulwark of woman's slavery."[45] At one time she wrote in a semi-humorous, semi-serious vein that "I did not attend the prayer meeting, for, as Jehovah has never taken a very active part in the suffrage movement, I thought I would stay at home and get ready to improve the committee."[46] Mrs. Stanton did not limit the sins of the church to the suppression of women, but protested that in general it supported the powerful and well-to-do as against the great majority.

Mrs. Stanton's religious beliefs went so far toward the unconventional as to include a sort of Freudian analysis—of course before the coming of Freud. She contended "that the feminine side of humanity, being the devotional and affectional, evolves the masculine God, as each sex worships its opposite. In worshipful men, the feminine predominates, hence the religions have been of the masculine type. The love of Jesus, among women in general, all grows out of sexual attraction. The Virgin Mary appeals in the same way to her male worshippers."[47] With her usual disregard of minor discrepancies, Mrs. Stanton did not explain why she had changed her mind about the emotionalism of women, or how her new concepts could be correlated with her argument that religion had been a male development to enslave women.

Mrs. Stanton spent her life crusading for what she considered the inalienable rights of women, although her definition of inalienable rights was not the usual one: "I am a disciple of the new philosophy that man's wants make his rights. I consider my right to property, to suffrage, etc., as natural and inalienable as my right to life and to liberty. Man is above all. The province of law is simply to protect me in what is mine."[48] The broadness of Mrs. Stanton's aims raises the question of why her major efforts were devoted to the attainment of only one small, specific object—the suffrage. The answer is a tribute to her essential practicality. She realized that a broadly conceived drive for feminine equality would be

61

a diffuse operation, involving many and often conflicting aims, and uniting all sort of opposition. A specific and limited objective would permit more concentrated effort and have greater chance of success. Her own arguments for suffrage were simple and impressive. She held that women were human beings and citizens, and that as such had a natural right to vote. If women voted, she continued, they could obtain whatever other forms of equality they desired, while their superior morals would raise the entire tone of American politics and lead to the elimination of such old ills as drunkenness.

Opponents of woman suffrage argued vociferously that most women did not want to vote, and Mrs. Stanton replied hotly that basic human rights should not be dependent on a majority vote: would you wait to educate your children, she asked, until they gave a majority vote for schools? And yet Mrs. Stanton was well aware of the truth and force of the opposing argument, and from time to time would express her unhappiness in some such statement as "In the indifference, the inertia, the apathy of women lies the greatest obstacle to their enfranchisement."[49] Obviously this story was considerably different from the contention that men were enslaving women, but again the propagandist was not too much concerned with minor lapses in logic. After all, Mrs. Stanton's basic concepts that men and women should be equal, but that women were superior, had in itself certain awkward implications.

The ideas of Mrs. Stanton naturally stirred opposition, which at times approached the scurrilous. Even the proposal that women should vote inspired dire predictions of family discord and the collapse of the American family, while the suggestion that men and women should have equality in all aspects of life evoked horrified responses in long and bitter diatribes. Although Mrs. Stanton's religious nonconformity was in general kept under cover, her ideas about marriage were not. Particularly well known were her proposals for easy divorce, which she publicized widely; the reactions of all conservatives, and particularly of those who were strongly religious, can be imagined.

The opposition to the Stanton views might superficially be expected to have labeled Mrs. Stanton as a dangerous radical to be avoided by all decent people, but actually there was no such reaction. Mrs. Stanton was personally attractive and plausible, so that even those who disagreed with her were likely to think kindly of this motherly, happy-looking woman. Then, too, she lived to a ripe old age, and during these years public sentiment was moving in the direction of what she had been advocating for so many years. Increasing numbers of men and women accepted the desirability of giving women more opportunity, even though many of them stopped far short of her ideals. The result was that Mrs. Stanton increasingly became an American landmark about which to boast, even if not to accept entirely.

As Mrs. Stanton grew older her physical strength declined, and she viewed with more pleasure the prospect of sitting in a rocking chair and dandling her grandchildren on her knees than that of attending conventions and making speaking tours. As she wrote to Olympia Brown, "The word 'go' has lost all charm for me."[50] After threatening several times to retire as president of the NAWSA, in 1892 she finally put down her foot: "Under no circumstances would I accept any office in any association. I want to be free of all anxiety & friction."[51] Quite naturally the mantle of the presidency of the NAWSA was transferred to the shoulders of her dear friend and lifetime co-worker, Susan B. Anthony.

Mrs. Stanton's eightieth birthday was marked by a national celebration, of which the high point was a gathering on November 12, 1895, at the Metropolitan Opera House in New York. When Mrs. Stanton, supporting herself on a cane, moved to the speaker's platform, she was greeted by an ovation. At the end of her speech the audience stood, cheered, and gave her the chautauqua salute of waving handkerchiefs. The tribute was well deserved. Mrs. Stanton had been the outstanding feminist of the past half century. While the contention may be advanced that social developments would have occurred in a similar fashion regardless of the work of any single individual, there is more merit in the argument that Mrs. Stanton made a greater contribution to the expansion of the opportunities of women than any other American.

4
Susan Brownell Anthony

Susan B. Anthony had the great misfortune to live most of her life in the shadow of Elizabeth Cady Stanton. Through almost all of her public career it was Mrs. Stanton who was the perennial president or chairman, while Miss Anthony sat farther back on the platform as vice-president or secretary. When they traveled together, as happened frequently, Mrs. Stanton made the principal speech, while Miss Anthony completed the necessary local arrangements, checked on the heating and decorations of the hall, and collected the money. Not until 1892, when Mrs. Stanton refused to continue her official responsibilities, did Miss Anthony become president of the National American Woman Suffrage Association.

The lesser prominence of Susan Anthony was a product of both physical and mental characteristics. Even in personal appearance she was at a disadvantage. While Mrs. Stanton appeared as plump, cheerful, motherly, and well groomed, Miss Anthony was tall, dark, angular, awkward, bespectacled, care-lined, and harried-looking. She suffered from a slight case of strabismus, and when she had an operation to straighten her right eye it actually turned a trifle the other way. While the defect was practically unobservable, she was very self-conscious about it and tried to have all her pictures in profile. She dressed neatly, but was never really interested in clothes, and, not having the figure to wear them effectively, often appeared as dowdy or downright shabby. Even her voice was inferior to that of Mrs. Stanton. In fact, everything seemed to conspire to keep her in second place, and Miss Anthony could in appearance have served as the model for the usual caricature of a feminist as an unattractive and soured old maid who was venting her spleen against men because they had ignored her.

The characterization of unattractive old maid was in fact completely unjustified for either Miss Anthony or for her friends who worked with her to further the rights of women. Most of the feminists were married and had children, and while Miss Anthony herself remained a spinster, it was by personal preference and not because of lack of numerous opportunities for marriage. Miss Anthony's appearance was a trifle intimidating, but was soon offset by her sweetness, her kindly disposition, and her friendly nature. The first reaction by a new acquaintance might well be relief that she was a "womanly woman,"[1] rather than the vinegary battle-axe which she had braced herself to encounter; the original fears were soon lost completely. Miss Anthony loved other people and they returned her affection; many of them have left records of that fact. Above all, she was straightforward and honest, with an extraordinarily good memory and with high moral standards of truth; an auditor could accept every statement as true and every promise as binding. She had a well-developed sense of humor, which persisted in spite of a frequently unfavorable environment; a record of her participating in charades as a passenger on a train seems hard to credit without an appreciation of a basic playfulness. Miss Anthony particularly adored small children, and was loved in return. She was helpful to younger workers for the cause, who brought her many of their personal problems, as well as questions of public tactics. Since these young women found "Miss Anthony" an overformal style of address, and "Susan" too familiar, they usually compromised on "Aunt Susan."

The main affliction of Miss Anthony was probably her health. She wrote innumerable letters detailing her physical distresses, and experimented with all sorts of medicines and diets. Although some considerable part of her illnesses may have been imaginary, there was no imagination regarding the suffering and anxiety caused by her teeth. For many years they gave her considerable pain, and her difficulties continued even after she had them removed, because her plates were never comfortable.

Physical complaints, when added to a sensitive and introspective nature, may have explained Susan Anthony's periodic fits of depression, when she was discouraged about both the present and future. For example, after a long fight in Nebraska she despaired of winning any popular votes in the states because, as she put it, "The *average* intelligence gets no higher!!"[2] At one time she wailed to Mrs. Stanton: "Mrs. Stanton, I have *very weak moments*—and long to lay my weary head somewhere and nestle my full soul close to that of another in full sympathy—I sometimes fear that *I too* shall faint by the wayside and drop out of the ranks of the faithful few."[3]

An introspective nature which entailed frequent periods of depression may have been responsible for Miss Anthony's philosophical gropings, which included attractions toward astrology, spiritualism, and theosophy. Religiously, she continued to accept through her life the existence of a future world, about which she quoted the words of her father on his deathbed,[4] but as she grew older her ideas lost much of their early precision. She believed, as did Mrs. Stanton, in the universality of natural law, and hoped that if she lived the best life of which she was capable the future would be satisfactory. But whatever her questionings and depressions, she kept them to herself and to her few most intimate friends, objecting even to the publication by her friend Mrs. Stanton of her Bible, which she called "flippant and superficial."[5]

Miss Anthony's speeches were not as effective as those of Mrs. Stanton. The typical Stanton speech was broadly conceived, beautifully developed, and effectively delivered. Miss Anthony, on the other hand, worried over her public appearances; copies of her speeches show a multiplicity of corrections. She did not have the assurance of her friend, and this lack of self-confidence had the effect of making her audiences less responsive. Later in life, after tremendous amounts of experience, she gained confidence, usually spoke extemporaneously, and sometimes produced a real emotional impact.

The most decisive characteristic of Susan B. Anthony was her wholehearted devotion to what she considered her duty, and she stated her point of view quite clearly in a speech which she titled "Expediency": "The soul that would be a true medium of *Gods Sunlight,* must keep itself unstained by cowardice,—must possess itself of the spirit of heroism that will dare to follow whenever & wherever it shall direct."[6] Susan Anthony devoted every ounce of her energy to the causes she felt to be right, regardless of criticism and hostility, and likewise regardless of the fact that other less dedicated women fell by the wayside. No woman has ever been more completely committed to the reform of the world.

Susan B. Anthony was born in western Massachusetts. Her mother, a Baptist in religion, was morbid on the subject of sex. She was always embarrassed when she was pregnant, isolated herself as much as possible, and never permitted any reference to her condition. Father Anthony, a Quaker, loomed very large in Susan's life, reminding one of the situation of Elizabeth Stanton. He was a man of strong moral and religious convictions, a thoroughgoing reformer whose particular hates were liquor, tobacco, and slavery. He was so stubbornly independent in his thinking that the church ultimately ejected him for refusal to conform, whereupon he became a Universalist. These traits may be seen repeated in his daughter, who most of her life thought of her father as the shining knight in white armor, the one perfect representative of his sex.

The Anthony family was moderately well-to-do when Susan was a girl, and since Susan was mentally precocious gave her a fine education for the day, culminating in a good Philadelphia school. Susan was even more conscientious and religious than other girls of her age and perpetually felt herself guilty of such

68

great sins as idle conversation, reflecting sadly that very possibly her heart was so hardened that she could not appreciate fully her own defects. She prayed that her heart might become "more and more refined until nothing shall remain but perfect purity."[7]

At the end of her schooling, Susan decided to earn her living by teaching, which was particularly desirable because by this time her father had little money, and the family had moved to a farm near Rochester, New York. In fact, she turned over part of her pay to the family. As an intelligent and well-educated young lady she advanced in her teaching until she was head of the girls' department of a secondary school at Conajoharie, New York. She retained her intensely moral outlook and a somewhat youthful intolerance for the foibles of her elders. She objected to the fashionable clothes upon which she felt too many women set their hearts. She criticized severely President Van Buren, who she charged reveled in luxuries, including the theater and the debasing wine, while little children cried for food. Abby Kelley felt that Susan Anthony grew intellectually during this period, and became "an exceedingly interesting woman,"[8] but there may be some question as to the general acceptability of Miss Kelley's criteria.

The Conajoharie period of the Anthony life was also notable for Miss Anthony's one and only venture into social life of a frivolous sort. She dropped the "plain language" of the Quakers, and became interested in clothes, writing in her diary of such intriguing garments as a pearl straw gypsy hat, decorated with white ribbons, fringe, roses, and green leaves; a gown of purple, white, blue, and brown plaid, with puffs around waist and skirt; blue prunella gaiters with patent-leather trimmings; watch, gold chain, and pencil; and big shell combs. While never beautiful, she was quite attractive with her slender, erect figure, her brown hair, and her regular features. Various swains escorted her to the social events of the area, and she even dreamed of marriage.

But Susan Anthony never married. Various explanations have been advanced, but none includes a lack of opportunity, since she had proposals even late in life. The most usual statement is that she was deterred by the experience of a beloved cousin who died as a consequence of childbirth, leaving four small children. This explanation seems inadequate, since the incident occurred when Susan was approaching thirty, and by this time her spinsterhood had become well established. At earlier times she had dreamed of marriage, but had always repented the next day; her comments on men stressed their lack of high morals, which may have meant that she was comparing them with her idolized and idealized father. Mrs. Stanton later remarked that in the years she had known Miss Anthony (since 1851), her friend had never shown any personal and romantic interest in any man. Since Miss Anthony was a normal woman, both mentally and physically, as far as can be determined, and had a great love for small children, the speculation comes naturally to mind that her failure to marry had some relation to the deeply emotional feeling she had toward her father. Since a dead woman cannot be psychoanalyzed, the accuracy of this speculation cannot be tested.

As she grew older Miss Anthony seemed to develop a more and more hostile attitude toward marriage. Writing of the professional training of a young friend she predicted a great future for her unless she should be caught in "the trap of matrimony, from which Good Lord deliver her."[9] The future, held Miss Anthony, was to be "AN EPOCH OF SINGLE WOMEN," for "the woman who WILL NOT BE RULED,—*must live without marriage.*" But these single women, continued Miss Anthony, must have homes of their own, because "A HOME OF OUR OWN is the soul's dream of rest."*[10] The depth of the Anthony feeling is attested not only by the frequent underlining, but by the many changes and corrections of the speech from which these

---

* The original letter underlines once the words in italics and twice those in small capitals.

words come. To some extent the Anthony writings indicate a laudation of women and a depreciation of men. While she said about women, "All of them are equally dear to me!!"[11] she made no equivalent statement about men.

Whether Susan Anthony was an effective teacher is uncertain, but certainly she had doubts of her own abilities, and lost interest: "A great weariness has come over me."[12] She wished she were a man so that she could follow the Gold Rush to California, but, being a woman, the best she could do was to devote her life to reform, which at first meant particularly temperance and abolition, since she was not as yet dedicated to the cause of women's rights. She established her home at Rochester (1850), where it remained the rest of her life, and did much housework in the intervals between her reforming efforts, since her mother's health was delicate and her sister taught.

Susan Anthony's early reform activities were concerned largely with temperance, a cause in agreement with her father's views and one considered a quite proper activity for a philanthropically minded woman. When Miss Anthony heard of the actions of the Seneca Falls convention she approved them in general, since she herself was a career woman who deplored the lower pay given to women, but she had one reluctance. Her conscience held that a person should not vote in a government that waged war. In any case, however, she felt no inspiration to offer her services in behalf of women's rights.

Another critical point in Susan Anthony's life came in 1851, when she first met Elizabeth Stanton. As Mrs. Stanton later told the story, Miss Anthony had been attending a temperance convention at Syracuse, and on her way home had stopped at Seneca Falls to visit her friend Amelia Bloomer and to hear William Lloyd Garrison. The two women met on the street and were introduced by Mrs. Bloomer. Mrs. Stanton was strongly impressed by Miss Anthony—particularly by "her good, earnest face and genial smile." She added: "I liked her thoroughly from the beginning."[13] So great was the impression that years later Mrs. Stanton could describe Miss Anthony's dress in detail; both Mrs. Stanton and Mrs. Bloomer were wearing the bloomer costume.

Soon the Stanton-Anthony friendship became one of the most important characteristics of the feminist movement. Miss Anthony often visited her friend's home, and sometimes took care of the children while their mother went on speaking trips. As the children grew older, Mrs. Stanton and Miss Anthony were almost continually in each other's company as they attended conventions and went on lecture tours. The reluctance of Miss Anthony to endorse suffrage for women was soon overcome, and she accepted it as the most desirable immediate goal. Many years later Lucy Stone's daughter asserted that her mother had converted Miss Anthony by a very convincing letter, but as level-headed a person as Carrie Chapman Catt doubted the truth of the story;[14] and certainly it seems more reasonable to think that the influence was that of Mrs. Stanton.

Miss Anthony's work of the early 1850's stressed temperance more than women's rights, but the two were closely connected. The common assumption of all temperance advocates, including Miss Anthony, was that practically all the drunkards were men and all the sufferers women. Every possible ounce of bathos was utilized in picturing the terrible plight of the poor wife and mother without legal recourse who was mistreated by a drunken brute of a husband. Miss Anthony went so far as to insist that such an unfortunate wife should refuse to have children by her disreputable husband, whereupon the newspapers expressed shocked horror that a presumably chaste maiden lady should discuss the intimacies of married life. Possibly they felt that such a lady, even if she no longer believed in the stork, should not admit her lapse from perfect innocence. At any rate, temperance speeches such as those of Miss Anthony made perfectly clear that women were more moral than men and that giving them the vote would hasten the day of state prohibitory laws.

Women in the temperance movement had experiences similar to those of women in the abolition movement. In fact, they were often the same women. As they attended temperance meetings, they discovered that men held all the jobs and made all the speeches; one often-quoted male has been reported as saying: "The sisters are not invited there to speak but to listen and to learn."[15] Red-blooded women who wanted to deliver their own messages and occupy at least the fringes of the spotlight could hardly accept this subordination. Sometimes they formed their own separate groups, but they still battled for a more prominent part in societies dominated by men. As Miss Anthony protested indignantly: "Has not God given us souls, reason? Was it meant she should be silent?"[16] The truth was that the men in this case were fighting a war which had practically been lost. At the world temperance convention at New York in 1853, which was so important that it dominated the news of the *Times* for several days,[17] there was a bitter battle over the women delegates, just as there had been in London in 1840, but this time the conservatives lost decisively. Secretary of the convention was Susan B. Anthony.

The profession of teaching also gave an opening to the growing Anthony feminism. During a state teachers' convention at Rochester in 1853 she observed that although two-thirds of the delegates were women, every speech during the first two days was delivered by a man. Ultimately her indignation came to a boiling point, and she rose and asked permission to speak. The result was great confusion, but she remained standing beside her chair until she had received permission by a narrow majority. Her speech did nothing to create more joy. She pointed out clearly and bitterly that as long as women were held incompetent to enter any other profession than teaching, male teachers would be held in disrespect as mentally inferior. The assembly was disturbed and even horrified; ultimately it voted that women should participate equally in future conventions and that the pay of women teachers was too low.

As the years passed, Miss Anthony devoted more and more of her attention to women's rights. Her first convention was in September 1852 at Syracuse, where she was one of the secretaries. Soon she was the most diligent worker in the cause, attending innumerable meetings, doing outside speaking, and writing hundreds of letters. Her diligence and efficiency brought the usual result of being saddled with more than her fair share of the detailed and discouraging jobs which no one desired. She wore herself out arranging for halls, distributing hand bills, collecting money, and planning meetings. The arranging of speakers was a particularly nasty detail, since all the women wanted to make speeches, but many either were not competent or would not spend the necessary time in preparation. As she wrote to Caroline Dall: "I do not wish to be rude or unkind, but I was so tired last year with rambling *undigested talk* from the women, that you will pardon me I know."[18]

Possibly Miss Anthony's greatest distress came from "the dearth of active workers,"[19] and she felt that women could be more easily persuaded to work for men than to labor to remove their own chains: "If we wanted them to do the *herculean task* for negro *men*—Irish *men* or any *class* of the *superior sex*—they would all, as one earnest woman, rush to the work—but for *themselves*—they seem so listless—it is hard to keep in the patience with them."[20]

The worst kowtowing to men, however, was that of the married feminists to their husbands. All too frequently the married women were absorbed by the *"ineffable joys of maternity,"*[21] and while Miss Anthony realized that as a spinster she had more free time than most of her colleagues, she still complained bitterly that no woman seemed able to withstand the matrimonial maelstrom. Speaking of her fellow feminists she wrote: "It does vex me to see our women tie themselves hand or foot with children. Women who can't do our work can bear or adopt babies—and that better than our women. So I say let those others do that work."[22] Such a statement implies a rather critical attitude toward marriage.

The Anthony conscience and logic inevitably brought the adoption of the bloomer costume, for Miss Anthony argued that women would never be independent until they adopted clothes that would permit them to compete with men on a basis of equality. Unfortunately, her experiences as "a Bloomer" were even more trying than those of others. Her tall, awkward figure, draped in baggy pants, was highly conspicuous, and her sensitive soul writhed in agony as she heard audible comments about "my Bloomer." She resented deeply the comments of "coarse brutal man," and time after time returned home to cry bitterly over her tribulations. When she told her troubles to Mrs. Stanton, her friend advised her: "I hope, Susan, you have let down a dress and petticoat. The cup of ridicule is greater than you can bear."[23] But in spite of this advice, Miss Anthony's conscience did not permit her to abandon the costume for another year. She never suffered more deeply for the cause.

Miss Anthony joined her friends in support of the North during the Civil War, but only after conquering conscientious qualms because of the ingrained Quaker hostility to war. At the end of the hostilities she went back to her efforts for women's rights, supporting loyally the leadership of Mrs. Stanton. In many ways a turning point of the work was a tour through Kansas in 1867 to win support for a constitutional amendment giving the vote to women. The Stanton-Anthony party was followed by a Lucy Stone group, and their plea was backed by Governor Robinson, but it lost decisively. More important for feminism, however, was the injection of George Francis Train into the proceedings, and the resulting disaffection among the women.

After Miss Anthony had returned from the losing Kansas

campaign she wrote to her friend Olympia Brown: "But don't despair—we shall win—the day breaks—the eastern sky is *red*."[24] That redness presumably was the new periodical *Revolution,* financed with Train money, which appeared early the next year. At its masthead were the words: "Principle, not policy; justice, not favors.—Men, their rights and nothing more: women, their rights and nothing less." Quite naturally, Mrs. Stanton was the editor and Miss Anthony did the dirty work.

Any reformist woman's periodical of the period was destined to have difficulties, but *Revolution,* besides being not a very good paper, was established in a particularly bad time in the history of American feminism. The women wanted to attach an expansion of their own rights to those of the Negro. The men reformers objected to the combination, with the result that the single-minded Miss Anthony was sure that the men hated her paper and wanted to kill it: "Every one of them, as far as I can learn, most heartily wishes the Revolution dead—*dead*—DEAD*—and would murder it at any minute had they the power."[25]

Troubles never came singly. After the Kansas failure and the problems created by *Revolution* came the split of the feminist camp into two rival organizations, and then the Beecher case and the Woodhull troubles. As for *Revolution,* Train soon withdrew his support and it collapsed, leaving Miss Anthony holding the financial bag. While she was not legally responsible, her overactive conscience forced her to spend the next years in paying off the debts of the infant money-loser. For the only time in her life Miss Anthony negotiated carefully for payments for her appearances, which at other times she had been willing to donate without charge.

Miss Anthony had other troubles during the same period— troubles of her own devising. While her paper was still alive

---

* The manuscript underlines the last word twice, the preceding word once.

she held weekly meetings in New York to discuss the various problems confronting women. These meetings attracted a considerable number of crackpots, including believers in free love, and hence brought very undesirable public reactions. In one sense, of course, they were praiseworthy as the free expression of individual opinions, and the NWSA was always more sympathetic to diverse ideas than the AWSA, but the adverse public opinion more than canceled the advantages. The trouble was further increased as *Revolution* opened its columns to all sorts of material, including a discussion of the very delicate subject of prostitution; the general attitude of the paper apparently was that prostitution was mainly the result of the seduction of pure women by wicked men. Odd words were printed about chastity: "Chastity is the natural inheritance of woman, and there is no particular merit in its possession, save when it has withstood the test of temptation."[26] One cannot help wondering whether these words were written by Miss Anthony and whether they referred to personal experiences.

Most important of the Anthony mistakes was the introduction of economic considerations in a discussion that was sufficiently acrimonious without them. In spite of Mrs. Stanton's realistic warnings against possible troubles, Miss Anthony felt that she had no choice but to express her sentiments in her usual straightforward way. She believed—and said continually—that economic independence was the real basis for the expansion of the rights of women: "What woman most needs is a true appreciation of her womanhood, a self-respect which shall scorn to eat the bread of dependence."[27] As to the possibility that economic equality would masculinize women, she felt that while such a result was unlikely, it would only show God's intention. Time after time she emphasized her conviction that a woman who was dependent on some man for even food, clothes, and shelter could never really be free. Man under such circumstances was inevitably a tyrant, and Miss Anthony never admitted like some of her co-workers that the situation might ever be reversed. She was pro-woman, as were others, but there was also about her writings a slight aura of an anti-man sentiment.

Women should at least be able to earn their own livings, and then, thought Miss Anthony, they should unite to raise their wages to the male level. Her main attack was to support a Workingwoman's Association to promote the needs of women earning their livings, but she went so far at one time as to urge women to advance themselves by taking the jobs of men on strike. Mrs. Stanton was worried about the implications of such work, and suggested that her friend confine herself to organizing suffrage groups, with the idea that suffrage was the necessary condition precedent to economic improvement, but Miss Anthony shrugged away the suggestion; this disagreement was very possibly the most serious the two women ever had. Miss Anthony may well have been right in theory, but Mrs. Stanton was certainly correct in terms of tactics. The Anthony work only slowed down the suffrage drive by creating confusion and division, and by encouraging greater opposition.

Miss Anthony's main efforts in the generation after the Civil War were in the direction of woman suffrage. To this end she worked herself beyond the limits of her physical strength. She attended dozens of conventions, made hundreds of speeches, and wrote innumerable letters. She traveled almost continuously, often under the worst of conditions, sometimes stopping at her Rochester home only long enough to catch her breath and wash her clothes. The center of her interest, and also the focus for the NWSA, was Washington. She did much lobbying and spoke before several Congressional committees, her addresses being delivered often with passionate earnestness. What is frequently forgotten is that a perceptible proportion of Congress, headed by George W. Julian of Indiana, was pro-woman suffrage. Indeed, possibly as many men as women throughout the nation favored votes for women.

The great objective of Miss Anthony and her friends was a sixteenth amendment to the Constitution to provide that "the right of citizens of the United States to vote shall not be denied or abridged by the United States or by any State on account of sex."[28] This amendment appeared before every Congress, and in time became known as the Susan B. Anthony Amendment. In considering this long fight for woman suffrage, one should bear in mind that suffrage never was regarded as the final goal, but only as the push that would open to women the doors of complete freedom and equality.

Miss Anthony was generally straightforward and prosaic, but at times she could become emotional, and even dramatic. At the Philadelphia Centennial of 1876, when Mrs. Stanton was refused the privilege of presenting a women's protest after the reading of the Declaration of Independence, Miss Anthony headed a group of women who marched down the aisle at the proper moment, distributed copies of their protest to the audience, and then read it from the platform, to the great distress of the presiding dignitaries. Miss Anthony was delighted to have women refuse to pay their taxes because they did not have votes, and regretted that she could not participate in such action because she did not possess any real property.[29]

The greatest Anthony publicity came from an incident which she described in a letter to Mrs. Stanton: "Well I have been & gone & done it!!—positively voted the Republican ticket—Strait—this A. M. at 7 oclock."[30] She and several other women registered and voted in Rochester during the election of 1872, apparently confusing and overawing the election inspectors. Several weeks later they were arrested by an embarrassed marshal for illegal voting, and indicted. Miss Anthony wanted to refuse to give bond, and stay in jail, but her lawyer overruled her. She spent her free time in making speeches in the area served by the court, whereupon the trial was moved to Canandaigua. Thus challenged, she made twenty-one speeches in twenty-two days in the Canandaigua region.

The first woman to be tried (June, 1873) was the acknowledged ringleader, Susan Anthony. Her defense was that women had been given the vote by the Fourteenth Amendment, and that even if this contention were wrong, she had committed no criminal offense. The judge, obviously convinced of her guilt before the trial started, refused to allow the accused to give evidence on her own behalf, and ultimately instructed the jury to bring in a verdict of guilty. He refused a new trial with a jury decision. And then, having carefully kept Miss Anthony quiet during the proceedings to date, he made the mistake of asking her whether she had any statement to make before sentence was passed. She responded immediately: "I have many things to say," and proceeded to say them in spite of frantic poundings of his gavel by the judge. Ultimately he was able to insert his judgment of $100 and costs. This experience must have scared him, for the other women were never tried. Each guilty election inspector was fined $25 and costs.

The fine was far from the end of the case. Miss Anthony refused to pay it, having an eye on a jail sentence, but the judge warily refused to make her a martyr. Then she petitioned Congress for remission of the fine, and her petition was considered by a committee of each house. The Senate Judiciary Committee felt that the federal government had no jurisdiction, but went so far as to recommend that Congress express its disapproval of the methods of the trial. Ultimately President Grant issued a pardon.

Susan Anthony attained the highest post in the women's movement, the presidency of the NAWSA, in 1892, but by this time she was getting older and losing some of her physical power. She continued to write and to attend meetings, and even had enough initiative to attend her first horse race, but once she lost her power of speech for a while, and from time to time she fainted. By 1895 her weakness was so evident that her friends urged her to slow down, and planned a steady income for her in case she could no longer earn her own. Ultimately (1899) she was herself persuaded, and planned to give up her presidency. As she looked around the world which greeted the new century, she was hopeful of the future. She felt that women were increasing in strength, self-reliance, independence, perception, and energy, and that they were selectting their husbands with greater intelligence.[31] She held that "the day will come when man will recognize woman as his peer, not only at the fireside, but in the councils of the nation. Then, and not until then, will there be the perfect comradeship, the ideal union between the sexes, that shall result in the highest development of the race."[32]

Quite fittingly, Susan Anthony ended life as she had lived it, in the service of women's rights. Rising from a sick bed to attend a convention, she contracted pneumonia at the meeting, but was able to get home, where she died quietly in her bed. She had spent half a century in single-hearted devotion to women's rights, and she had the satisfaction to live sufficiently long to see many of her goals in the process of realization.

5
Lucy Stone

LUCY STONE was one more woman who started as an Abolitionist and ended as a worker for feminism. She was remembered widely for many years because she retained her maiden name after her marriage and because followers of the same practice were called "Lucy Stoners." Time has dimmed this claim to distinction as the practice of retaining the maiden name has become more frequent, but Lucy Stone is still remembered as one of the outstanding contributors to the agitation for women's rights.

Lucy Stone was a partisan of increased rights for women almost from her birth. She was born on a farm in Massachusetts, run by her father Francis, a prosperous farmer and tanner and also a domineering man who insisted vigorously upon the superiority of the male sex. Her mother Hannah was meek, docile, and self-effacing, raising at least no audible objections to her husband's dogmatic views. Lucy sympathized with her mother and felt hostile to her father. At the same time she knew at first hand the difficult work of a woman because while still a girl she took over responsibility for the family at various times when her mother was sick. Though Lucy was healthy, vigorous, truthful, energetic, intelligent, and generally happy, she was deeply saddened by what she felt to be the unhappy fate of women, particularly in marriage, and promised herself that she would never marry.

Lucy Stone was greatly shocked to learn as she grew older that the Bible lent authority to the suppression of women and to the view that they are inferior. At first she concluded that even God had forgotten them, but then she argued to herself that very possibly the men who had translated the Bible had made changes to buttress their own claims of superiority. The answer to this duplicity of men was to learn Latin and Greek, which she felt would enable her to read the Scriptures in the original. Learning Latin and Greek meant college, and her father was horrified at the idea. He was no miser and was perfectly willing to pay for college educations for his sons, but, since the idea of college for a girl was beyond his comprehension, he refused to contribute a cent to the foolhardy scheme. Being extremely persistent, at the age of sixteen Lucy began to teach district school and to save from her small wages. Periodically she interrupted her teaching to attend various secondary schools, including Mount Holyoke, to prepare herself further for advanced education.

Nine years of drudgery were necessary before Lucy Stone felt able to enter Oberlin in the class of 1847, and even then she needed to live frugally and to do outside work to keep financially solvent. After two years of scrimping even her father agreed that she really wanted to go to college, and he contributed to her expenses for the remainder of his daughter's college career. One of her classmates later remembered her as attractive, bright, neat, and hard-working. Obviously he could have added that she was older than her classmates. At Oberlin she was influenced by President Charles G. Finney to become a Unitarian, although she was also affected by her keen awareness that her girlhood church, the Congregational, refused to permit women to vote.

After graduation, Miss Stone embraced neither teaching nor marriage, the two obvious options for an intelligent and well-educated girl. She had had enough of teaching and had promised herself never to marry. Instead, she started to work for abolition, and within a year was a regular representative of the anti-slavery society. Intensely serious and completely devoted to her subject, she toured the countryside, encountering the usual difficulties with rowdies who interrupted the meetings and even hurled various objects at her head.

Lucy Stone was an effective abolitionist speaker—in part because of her sex. She appeared before her audiences as a very attractive and magnetic woman—short, well-built, and completely feminine. Her rosy cheeks, her tipped nose, her bright gray eyes, her strong mouth with its excellent teeth, her masses of dark brown hair brought an immediately favorable response, which was heightened by her well-pitched and melodious voice. Everyone, friend and foe alike, praised her speaking in extravagant terms. Possibly it is ungracious to mention her two main defects. One was an almost total absence of humor; life for Miss Stone was desperately earnest, and the most vivid imagination fails to picture her telling a joke. The other defect was that she had very little to say. She lacked originality and was extremely doctrinaire, so that her speeches were merely rehashes of familiar abolitionist arguments. But then it should be added immediately that the rehashes were good, and very effective.

The Stone feminism was not very apparent during the 1840's, even though it obviously existed. Miss Stone devoted herself heart and soul to abolition, and agreed with her male co-workers that the woman issue should not be allowed to enter the abolition campaign, where it made progress more difficult.[1] During the 1850's she transferred her energies more and more to feminism, becoming one of the most active and best-known of the agitators. She issued the calls and made the arrangements for several of the national conventions, presided over some of them, and spoke at them almost continuously. Her friend T. W. Higginson's laudation that "Lucy is Queen of us all . . . and delights the whole country from Maine to Kentucky"[2] was a bit overenthusiastic, however, for though everyone agreed that Miss Stone spoke well, to the many who disagreed heartily with the doctrines she preached she was hardly a queen. Furthermore, Miss Stone did not increase the receptiveness of her audiences by adopting the bloomer costume, even though by common report she looked better than her pants-clad compatriots; one of her early costumes (1853) was described with no enthusiasm, as a short skirt with black "continuations."

The attitude of Lucy Stone toward feminine rights was in general that of her fellow workers. She was not an original thinker. Miss Stone's strong partisanship of women and her lack of humor led her even to urge that her female friends should consult women phrenologists rather than the popular Fowlers, who were men. Women, according to Miss Stone, desired rights rather than courtesies, and should have equality with men in all fields of activity. The vote was of course one of these rights, and taxation without representation was tyranny. Furthermore, women's higher moral standards would cleanse politics and eliminate all sorts of bad conditions, from brutish husbands to baby farming. More job opportunities should be available for women, and there should be equal pay for equal work.

Educational opportunities should be equal for men and women, with such schools as Yale and Harvard open to both sexes, since schools then admitting girls were characterized as inferior—a contention that could hardly have pleased her own alma mater, Oberlin. Coeducation was obviously desirable: "Brown and Amherst do not admit women. Hence the rowdyism. Coeducation would have made such behavior impossible. Witness Oberlin with half a century of open doors to women, and well-behaved students all the time."[3] Obviously Miss Stone was not an infallible prophet. In general she held that women should be given complete freedom to show their abilities, whether in the colleges or by work in the fields.

The Bible was a worrisome matter to Miss Stone from girlhood, and in her attitude she was more radical than most of her co-workers, even though her college education did not produce a new and different feminine translation of the Scriptures, as she had hoped. In fact, her literal mind accepted existing Scriptural passages exactly as they appeared, with no attempt at reinterpretation. She agreed that the Bible meant what it said when it told women to be submissive and wives to obey their husbands, but then pointed out that it had also told people to obey their rulers and that they had revolted. As to the injunction of Paul for wives to obey their husbands, Miss Stone held that the injunction no longer applied in this modern and enlightened age, and that in fact one could be sure that anything in the Bible contrary to woman's rights did not come from God. The clear implication that the individual should disregard any teaching of the Bible with which he did not agree was certainly a dangerous and subversive doctrine in the opinion of almost all religious Americans.

Marriage was also a matter of deep concern to Miss Stone, even though she urged as a matter of tactics that its discussion be excluded from the women's rights conventions.[4] She would become extremely emotional over the treatment of sweet, patient wives by brutish husbands: "One noble woman told me how she fled from her husband, to the *Shakers,* because he gave her no peace either during menstruation, pregnancy, or nursing."[5] Miss Stone was quite certain not only that wives should be given greater legal rights, but that every woman should learn to earn her own living, so that she would not be dependent upon marriage.

By her mid-thirties, Lucy Stone had apparently established permanently a satisfactory way of life for herself, there came to her a cataclysmic change. She fell in love. Here was a real perplexity. She had long been certain in her own mind that she would never marry, and now that belief tottered. So shattering was the change that she even acquired a new feeling of modesty, doubting that she could make her beloved happy. The object of her affections, Henry B. Blackwell, was ten years younger than she, and this difference of age was the basis for some of her questioning. Intellectual differences did not exist, for Henry agreed precisely with Lucy on such vital matters as abolition, woman's rights, and marriage. He was also a man of tact, pleasing his loved one with such gifts as a copy of Plato, and with such social activities as abolition meetings. His intelligent courting brought its well-merited reward of success.

The marriage of Lucy Stone and Henry Blackwell in 1855 was performed by their friend and fellow reformer T. W. Higginson, who described it as the "most beautiful bridal I ever attended."[6] Since the ceremony took place in the country, only close friends were invited; some of them, like Antoinette Brown and Elizabeth Blackwell, failed to arrive. Quite obviously the ceremony omitted the word *obey* from the bride's vows, and almost as naturally the bride and groom issued a joint statement beginning, "While we acknowledge our mutual affection . . ." and continuing to protest the current legal status of a wife.[7] What was more unusual was that Lucy Stone retained her maiden name as one further protest against the wife's legal subserviency, although sometimes for legal reasons she signed herself "Lucy Stone, wife of Henry B. Blackwell." Normally she was addressed as Mrs. Stone, which in itself was somewhat surprising, since her husband did not indicate his own marital status in his title. But regardless of these unusual trimmings, the marriage was a real love match, and at the end of the ceremonies Lucy broke down and wept "like any village bride."[8]

The Stone-Blackwell marriage was very happy. The partners were ideally mated, worshipping the same gods and having the same intense, moral, and idealistic temperaments. Appearances seem to indicate that Mrs. Stone was the dominant figure—possibly Henry should have called himself Mr. Lucy Stone. One of their first activities was to attend a woman's rights convention at Cincinnati in 1855, where Mrs. Stone could show off her new husband to her friends and fellow workers. And then, just like most brides, Mrs. Stone became pregnant. The child was Alice Stone Blackwell, born September 14, 1857, who became almost inevitably an ardent feminist and a passionate apologist of her mother, whom she supported at times with more emotion than good judgment. There is some evidence that as a girl she was at times difficult to control.

After the marriage, Lucy Stone naturally established her own home, and with the birth of the baby refused to accept outside speaking engagements, holding that the raising of a family was a full-time occupation.[9] She was an admirable wife and mother, diligent, clean, hard-working, and a good cook. Her main regret was that she had only one child. Her resolution to refuse outside engagements proved impossible to keep, however, and soon she was again working actively for the cause. During the Civil War she was president of the Woman's National Loyal League.

Even when Mrs. Stone remained at home she could still make news. When she received her tax bill in December 1857 she returned it unpaid with a letter that began: "Inclosed I return my tax-bill without paying it. My reason for doing so is that women suffer taxation and yet have no representation . . . ."[10] The local constable then had the unpleasant duty of selling sufficient Stone household goods to cover the taxes. They turned out to be a table and pictures of the Governor and of Gerrit Smith, which no doubt were a small price to pay for the dramatizing of the wrongs of women.

The troubles which struck the woman's rights movement at the end of the Civil War naturally found Lucy Stone in the eye of the hurricane. When the Stanton-Anthony group withdrew from the American Equal Rights Association and formed the NWSA, the Stone-Blackwell group had already gone home. Upon hearing the news, Mrs. Stone was greatly upset. She had understood Mrs. Stanton to say that she would take no such action and was naturally displeased that the new organization was dominated by New Yorkers, with many of her own friends absent. Moreover, she herself had been one of the best-known and most active of the feminists, and now she had not even been consulted, which meant that she had no influence in stating the objectives of the new group, and no official position.

The events of 1869 brought to a head the increasing coolness between the Stone and Stanton adherents. These differences involved mainly tactics and personalities rather than basic ideology. Mrs. Stanton's widely disseminated and libertarian views on divorce, and Miss Anthony's adventures in economic reform seemed to Mrs. Stone very unfortunate as creating diversions, involving a diversity of objectives. Even more immediately vital was the difference in attitude toward the Fifteenth Amendment. Mrs. Stanton was very bitter and called it a "new stab at womanhood," asserting that her "soul travailed in anguish,"[11] while Miss Anthony wailed that two million more men were being given tyrannical power over women. Mrs. Stone also objected to the terms of the Amendment, but felt that stressing this attitude would not only do no good but would actually hurt the women by antagonizing the male Abolitionists, who had generally favored women's rights. Part of the story was the Stanton-Anthony periodical *Revolution,* which disseminated the objectionable views, and which few women greeted with enthusiasm.

Mrs. Stone also felt strongly that some of the friendships of Mrs. Stanton and Miss Anthony were a handicap, particularly their association with George Francis Train. When the Stanton-Anthony-Train party toured Kansas in 1867, Mrs. Stone was horrified by the inclusion of a man with such a reputation "that no decent woman should be in his society."[12] Her friend Mrs. Mary Livermore called Train "a mill-stone round the neck of any cause."[13]

Unfortunately, a certain amount of personal friction was also involved. Most obvious was the hostility of Mrs. Stone toward Miss Anthony, a crisis being reached when Mrs. Stone accused Miss Anthony publicly of misusing organization funds. Miss Anthony was hurt deeply by the charge, and her mind reverted to it continually. But the situation was broader than the friction between these two leaders. Paulina Wright Davis wrote about "a party whose *purpose aim* and *object* is to destroy Elizabeth C. Stanton and S. B. Anthony,"[14] and while this type of charge was overemotional, it probably contained a basic truth. Involved in the situation was a conflict for power, and outsiders quite commonly thought of the dispute in terms of a fight between the New York and Boston groups for control.

The disagreements resulted in a call by the Stone-Blackwell people for the formation of a new woman's rights group. In addition to other reasons, the Boston people contended that the NWSA was not really national, that it excluded men, and that its meetings were confused mass assemblies; these were minor points and could hardly be supported effectively as long as the NWSA had barely been organized, and really had no record. The greatest feather in the Stone cap was persuading Gerrit Smith to join in the final call for a convention to establish a new organization. Mrs. Stone had been very clever by stressing the proposition that the new group would not oppose the Fifteenth Amendment. Mrs. Stanton was deeply wounded that a relative would apparently go over to the opposition, and worked very hard to get Smith to give his public support to the NWSA.

The Stone-Blackwell convention gathered at Cleveland in 1869. The most surprising attendant was Miss Anthony, who sat on the platform. She explained that "in case *too big* yarns—*too gross* misstatements of persons, principles, positions—I can just *help them state the truth*."[15] The convention organized the American Woman Suffrage Association, dedicated exclusively to the winning of suffrage. The Boston connection was minimized with the election of Henry Ward Beecher as president, and with the inclusion of G. W. Curtis and George Julian among the vice-presidents. Presumably Mrs. Stone herself could have been president if she had so desired.

The AWSA differed from the NWSA but slightly. It stuck a trifle more closely to the suffrage issue, and probably emphasized state work a little more than its rival, but the differences were certainly minor, and soon the younger workers lost even the faintest idea of the original distinctions. In general the AWSA outshone its rival in its early history. Its president, Henry Ward Beecher, was America's most popular minister, and while the NWSA countered with the romantic Theodore Tilton, Tilton could never match the appeal of his mentor. Both organizations were deeply unhappy when Tilton sued Beecher for the alienation of the affections of Mrs. Tilton and were glad to soft-pedal the story as much as possible.

One of the most important actions of the AWSA was the establishment of the *Woman's Journal,* which was to flourish from its start in 1870 until it was transformed to the *Woman Citizen* after the coming of the suffrage amendment. The *Journal* started with a real flair, even though later it was criticized severely as dull, timid, and uninspired. Its editorial board in the early years included Mrs. Stone, but the major work was done by Mrs. Mary Livermore, who was sufficiently important for the *Boston Transcript,* upon her death, to call her the "foremost woman in America."[16] Mary Livermore was a Boston girl, trained in the strict Calvinist tradition, and well educated. For some years she did teaching, and then in 1845 at the age of twenty-four she married a Universalist minister, Daniel P. Livermore. After various pastorates, the Rev. Mr. Livermore settled in Chicago (1857) as editor of the *New Covenant.* During the Civil War, Mrs. Livermore worked for the Sanitary Commission, first in Chicago and then in camps and hospitals. Her own account of her experiences is a long, dull, and amazingly garbled affair, which leads the reader to wonder how the writer could possibly have been efficient as an editor, and to marvel at the informal nature of the Civil War, in which a philanthropic woman was permitted to wander through the military installations, apparently

at her own whim. Maybe she overawed any possible interference by her regal appearance, for she was tall and commanding, with a large head, blue-gray eyes, and auburn hair.

During the Civil War, Mrs. Livermore came to the conclusion that woman suffrage was necessary to combat effectively such problems as liquor, poverty, and prostitution. In
earlier years her husband had been a more ardent supporter of
votes for women than she. With her new convictions she
started to edit a suffrage paper, the *Agitator* (1869), and from
this editorial job she was called to take charge of the new
Woman's Journal. In addition to her editing, she did a great
deal of lecturing in the next quarter century. In general, she
tended to be conservative rather than radical. She agreed
that most girls would spend their lives in marriage, and urged
that they be trained properly in coeducational schools, but
added that most household work should be simplified and
done coöperatively, to leave the wife more time for outside
activities. She worked hard for prohibition under the auspices
of the W. C. T. U. She deplored the immorality of such writers
as Oscar Wilde and Walt Whitman, feeling particular horror
if girls had Whitman's poems or even pictures of him in their
rooms. She supported the Spanish-American War even though
she opposed war in general. She did not delude herself with
the belief that women were panting for freedom. In fact she
held that women were interested mainly in pleasing men and
that "in order to get the women, we must first get the men."[17]
Even in her own day her views were generally conservative;
only the most reactionary of Americans would label her radical
because of her support of temperance and woman suffrage.

The last few years of Mrs. Livermore's life were pathetic.
Her health was none too good, and she had continual pain
from her eyes; in fact, she had been threatened with blindness
earlier in life. The death of her husband had left a gaping
void, and her attention was focused on the hope of reuniting
with him in the near future. In the meantime she consulted

mediums, and in time was able to announce that she had communicated with her husband. As she put it, "The world about me, at times, seems unreal and shadowy,"[18] and it must have been with relief and deep pleasure that she finally went to join her beloved husband (1905).

The divided feminist movement was a sad situation for many women who realized the desirability of united action, but efforts at reunion floundered continually on the rock of personal bitterness. As early as 1873, Mrs. Stone wrote to her friend T. W. Higginson, "I have received an astounding letter from your Mrs. Stanton begging me to lay aside my 'personal feud with Susan.' She asks me to 'give up my petty revenge.' "[19] Mrs. Stone then stated that the real trouble was that the *Woman's Journal* did not give enough coverage to the affairs of the NWSA. The personal bitterness behind this letter is quite obvious, with the clear implication that coöperation would be extremely difficult. Rather revealing was the fact that Mrs. Stanton made early overtures, demonstrating again her buoyant and extroverted nature, but in this case providing no tribute to her tactfulness. As late as 1889 Miss Anthony still wrote bitterly of "Lucy Stone & Co.," and insisted that any overtures for reunion come from Mrs. Stone.

The inevitable reunion finally came in 1890, the merged organization being called the National American Woman Suffrage Association. Mrs. Stone denied any interest in the presidency, expressing a preference for Miss Anthony over Mrs. Stanton. The vote resulted 131 to 90 for Stanton over Anthony, but Miss Anthony received the vice-presidency by an overwhelming 213 to 8. Mrs. Stone became chairman of the executive board.

By the latter part of her life Mrs. Stone had become something of a tradition. One starry-eyed future worker for the cause described her as "a calm, motherly-faced woman . . . in a dainty little white lace cap," with "one of the sweetest voices I ever heard."[20] This idyllic picture had little in common with

Mrs. Stone's well-known career as a passionate fighter of deep convictions. Her last speech was delivered at the Chicago Columbian Exposition in 1893, and from this appearance she returned home to die from a tumor. She had been an indefatigable fighter for what she considered right, and her influence had been considerable in the drive for expanded feminine opportunity.

6
The Literary Approach

ABOLITION WAS by no means the only road that led to feminism. Any active-minded woman who desired a career outside the home was a reasonable candidate for entertaining liberal ideas about the place of women in society, particularly if her youthful experiences predisposed her in that direction. While the most socially acceptable of these outside occupations was authorship, even here a woman might become aware of feminine disabilities. Furthermore, if she was a sensitive observer of life she had at least a reasonable chance of being impressed by the social and economic inequalities affecting her sex.

To imply that the usual woman author was a feminist would be a wild distortion of the truth. A woman like Grace Greenwood, who was both a popular author and an ardent feminist, was representative of only a small minority. For each Grace Greenwood there were a dozen Harriet Beecher Stowes and Mrs. E. D. E. N. Southworths, who were completely traditional in their social ideals. The usual woman author devoted herself almost completely to didactic tales for children, emotional tales of sentiment, hints for housewives, and romantic novels for sentimental misses who had no desire to read stark realism or to reform the world.

The general social conformity which characterized literature applied somewhat less in the field of journalism, where women's place was less secure. Mrs. J. C. Croly, for example, expressed her irritation at what she considered male discrimination by founding the feministic club Sorosis (1868), which later inspired the formation of the General Federation of Women's Clubs. A woman reporter or editor had a difficult struggle to

97

obtain her niche in the journalistic world, and might in consequence have at least a moderate tendency toward feminism.

The woman author was particularly visible in the half century before the Civil War, when she frequently dominated the lists of best sellers; the decade just prior to the war has frequently been labeled the "feminine 'fifties." A recent writer[1] has speculated that the obvious traditionalism of these pre-Civil War authors obscures a deeper and more significant revolt against men. She points out that the central and strongest characters in their books are almost always women, and that men have been reduced to unimportance and impotency. The point is made that the women authors were objecting subconsciously to the inferior position of their sex, and by their writings were compensating fictionally for the repressions of real life. Whether or not this explanation is justified, most women novelists would have denied vigorously any charge that they were feminists either consciously or unconsciously.

Of the women who combined literary careers with feminism, Lydia Maria Child is frequently mentioned as a pioneer. In point of fact, Mrs. Child was not only a very poor writer but an even poorer feminist; indeed her feminism was so mild that a microscope is necessary to find it. Lydia Maria Child was born Lydia Maria Francis, the daughter of a prosperous Massachusetts family which provided her a superior education. Maria, as she was usually known, did some teaching, but most of her life was spent in writing. Her first novel was written in six weeks and published when she was twenty-two. Both of these facts are evident in the poorly written and romantic tale of a white girl who thought her lover had died and so married an Indian, by whom she had a child; when the first lover proved to be still alive, the Indian husband quietly and heroically eliminated himself by means of an Indian divorce.

At the rather advanced age of twenty-six, Miss Francis married David Lee Child, a Harvard-educated lawyer who was an ardent Abolitionist, like Maria's father. Mrs. Child continued to write, partly because she liked it, and partly because David was more absorbed in promoting abolition than in providing for his family. Mrs. Child tried her hand at almost any kind of composition. For several years she edited a *Juvenile Miscellany,* and together with her husband edited an anti-slavery magazine. Most profitable were her several books of advice to women; her *The Frugal Housewife* went through forty editions. Her most deeply felt efforts were in support of abolition, although her writing was actually moderate in tone. In addition she did sketches, articles, poems, travel accounts, and history, including histories of women and of religious ideas; incidentally, her own religious beliefs were tolerant and nonsectarian, and included an interest in spiritualim. Possibly her most useful work was her *Letters from New York,* which was reasonably good description, and was particularly notable for its discussion of prostitution. At least Mrs. Child was not unbearably egotistical about her own work: "I believe I have done no harm by my writing, and I hope I have done some good."[2]

Mrs. Child's concern with women's rights was moderate. Her *The History of the Condition of Women, in Various Ages and Nations* (2 vols., 1835) was a storehouse of information, but did not support vigorously any positive and decided point of view. In general, Mrs. Child felt that there should be more equality between men and women, but her thought was that women at present had higher moral standards[3] and that men should try to attain similar excellence.[4] Women should be better educated, but primarily in domestic matters so that a bride would be more competent to run her home efficiently.[5] Her excitement about the whole matter was decidedly limited, however, because she felt that women's status was improving satisfactorily, as witness the increasing acceptance of women authors. For real emotional involvement one must read her lachrymose wails over that "brave old man" John Brown[6] or her condolences to his wife.

Much more of a feminist than Mrs. Child, and also more important as an author, was Sarah Margaret Fuller, who in spite of a marriage late in life is still almost always identified as Margaret Fuller. Margaret Fuller was another Massachusetts girl from a well-to-do family. Her father was a Harvard graduate and a lawyer, served both in the Massachusetts legislature and in Congress, and possibly in part as a result of this eminence was a bitter and exacting father.

As a girl, Margaret was awkward physically and precocious mentally. Her total education was superior. She started the study of Latin at the age of six, and learned to read the classics of eight languages, including Latin and Greek. On the other hand, she was emotionally unstable and subject while in boarding school to seizures of hysteria—related possibly to the advent of adolescence. Physically she was none too strong, being plagued by ill-health all her life. Reputedly she was "devoid of beauty and rather disagreeable,"[7] wore peculiar clothes, spoke with a nasal twang, and opened and closed her eyes incessantly. Even her admirer R. W. Emerson agreed that she "made a disagreeable first impression on most persons."[8]

At the conclusion of her schooling Margaret Fuller did some teaching, including a period at the very famous progressive school of Bronson Alcott. She soon came to know a large proportion of the eminent people who lived in the Boston area, including such well-known men as Emerson, Alcott, Parker, Thoreau, Ripley, and W. H. Channing. She was held in high respect by the intellectuals, especially by the Transcendentalists, who made her an editor of their magazine the *Dial*. Later in the 1840's she moved to New York to become literary editor of Horace Greeley's *New York Tribune*. Certainly she was an important person, and she proclaimed this fact loudly, for modesty was not one of her virtues. Assessing her own value she stated: "I now know all the people worth knowing in America, and I find no intellect comparable to my own."[9] Later commentators have been somewhat less admiring.

Miss Fuller's ideas about women were expressed in various writings, but their most elaborate presentation was in her book *Woman in the Nineteenth Century*. This book never sold well, and its failure has been credited by some to its excessively philosophical tone, but also can be explained by the unpopularity of its views, or by the excessive efforts at semantic cleverness, or by the flowery, diffuse, and often incomprehensible writing. Miss Fuller, like other proponents of her sex, rejected indignantly the idea that women should be the equals of men. In her opinion, such equality would mean a degradation of women except in the unlikely event that men raised their moral standards. Men were vain, fond of power, and generally dull, with superiority mainly as soldiers and lawyers. The only clear-cut male superiority was in physical strength, which had been overrated in importance and which certainly had no influence on the more important mental powers. The only proper equality of the sexes was in management of the home and in religion.

The special genius of woman was "to be electrical in movement, intuitive in function, spiritual in tendency,"[10] and the intuitive woman could usually leave the plodding male flat-footed in the search for truth. Miss Fuller was willing to agree that there was much overlapping in special sexual mental traits, with some intelligent men, since, as she put the situation, "There is no wholly masculine man, no purely feminine woman,"[11] but the generalization remained that women as a rule outshone the more pedestrian and stupid men.

Women should be given equal educational opportunities so that they might demonstrate their inherent superiority. Even assuming that the great majority of women would continue to spend most of their time in the stultifying environment of the home, they still needed sufficient education to enable them to be interesting to their husbands. Furthermore there were many women who for one reason or another did not have husbands, and these women needed proper training in order to earn their own livings. In this connection Miss Fuller sang a small paean of praise to the spinster, who was able to get along without male support. Possibly she had her own single-blessedness in the back of her mind.

Margaret Fuller moved in 1846 to Italy, where she fell in love with Angelo Ossoli, titled, handsome, penniless, dissipated, and younger than Margaret by ten years. A son was born to the couple on September 5, 1848, and a year later came the announcement that they were married, with the date unspecified. In 1850 Margaret Fuller and her son set sail for the United States, but their ship was wrecked, and both drowned. In spite of her relatively short life, Margaret Fuller had made a very considerable impression upon the United States, particularly on the small group which considered itself the intellectually elite of the young nation. Her long-run importance is more questionable. While she has inspired much research effort by scholars, and particularly by students of literature, her influence is hard to detect. In the feminist movement her writings were too abstract to be influential, and she never participated in the main stream of feministic agitation. Regretfully, the historian must conclude that her importance in the expansion of women's sphere was relatively small.

Jane Swisshelm was another woman inclined toward both literature and feminism, but in practically every other way she was vastly different from Mrs. Child and Miss Fuller. Instead of being Eastern-born she originated in what at the time seemed the West—western Pennsylvania. Her family was not well-to-do, and her father died while she was a small girl, so that her education was not so good as that of either Mrs. Child or Miss Fuller. On the other hand, she was similar to them in being a very religious girl, and in being precocious mentally. Because of the family finances she started to contribute to the family income at the age of ten, and ultimately tried various jobs, including teaching. Her life seemed to be following a quite normal pattern when she fell in love with a young farmer, James Swisshelm, married him just a short time before her twenty-first birthday, and settled down to housekeeping.

The Swisshelm marriage encountered serious difficulties almost at once. One trouble was the hostility of Jane's mother-in-law, but much more important were temperamental conflicts between husband and wife. James loved and admired his wife, but he was not well educated and was extremely conservative, with the strong belief that the husband should be dominant in the home, and insisted upon exhibiting his masculine superiority. Jane's frame of mind was more complex. She was young and very much in love with her husband, and tried her best to adjust her life to his ideas, going as far as to stop all outside activities and to give up all reading except the Bible so that she would not make her husband feel inferior. On the other hand, she always retained a basic individuality and stubbornness which never permitted the complete docility which apparently James would have preferred.

Possibly James had been deluded by Jane's appearance. She was a pretty little girl, only five feet tall and a hundred pounds in weight, with blue eyes, high forehead, and brown hair parted in the middle. She was quiet in manner and soft in voice, and her smile was engaging. Very easily, James might have acquired the idea that she was a malleable doll, but if such was the case, he was quite mistaken. Under the soft exterior were a strong will and decided opinions.

Troubles began to loom larger in 1838 when James tried to make his fortune by establishing a business in Louisville, Kentucky. For one thing, Jane saw slavery at first hand, and her passionate loathing tended more and more to dominate her thinking and her life. Equally important was the failure of James's business, which meant that Jane felt the desirability of helping the family income by teaching when they returned

103

North. Such outside work must have hurt deeply the traditionally minded husband, who undoubtedly felt himself a failure in the basic masculine responsibility of earning the family living.

Marital relations deteriorated rapidly. As Mrs. Swisshelm later told the story, the greatest single disagreement was over the mother, who became sick and wanted her daughter at her bedside. But James said "no," and Jane was torn between the conflicting injunctions of two Biblical statements: "Wives, obey your husbands," and "Children obey your parents." Ultimately she followed the latter. When her mother died, she left her estate to Jane and her sister, whereupon the husband threatened to sue the estate for the value of his wife's services while she nursed her mother.

Confronted with a difficult family situation, Mrs. Swisshelm found an outlet by writing short sketches and articles for the papers—at first under a pseudonym and then under her own name. Increasingly these writings were concerned with slavery. Ultimately she gained sufficient confidence in her abilities to undertake a little paper of her own, the weekly *Pittsburgh Saturday Visiter* [*sic*], of which she wrote the greater part herself, and which ultimately died in 1852. The main emphasis of the paper was on abolition, but it is hardly surprising that there crept into its columns objections to the status of women, and particularly of wives. At one time Mrs. Swisshelm described the position of a woman as something better than that of a baboon but lower than that of a Negro slave. Mrs. Swisshelm's writings were direct, vigorous, and pungent, tending to get beneath the skin of the reader. They were reprinted widely, so that the influence of the feeble Pittsburgh paper was much greater than might have been expected.

The spreading reputation of Mrs. Swisshelm in time reached the ears of Horace Greeley in New York, who commissioned her to report on the affairs of Congress for his *New*

York Tribune. The articles turned out to be very stimulating but completely unreliable. Mrs. Swisshelm's emotions were so thoroughly aroused by slavery that she found accurate reporting impossible.

The domestic friction of the Swisshelm family ultimately proved unendurable, and Jane deserted her husband. Curiously enough, the condition about which she apparently was most bitter was not her specific disputes with her husband but her lack of privacy in marriage. Taking her six-year-old daughter with her, she moved to Minnesota in 1857, and three years later her husband obtained a divorce on the ground of desertion. Mrs. Swisshelm established in her new home the *St. Cloud Visiter,* which was even more incendiary than her previous paper, and which inspired manifold troubles, including the burning of her press by a mob and threats on her life. She still found time and strength to do much lecturing. While at times she spoke of women's rights, her favorite subject was abolition. She favored the Greeley point of view on possible secession—that the erring sisters should be allowed to depart in peace.

When the war came, Mrs. Swisshelm was loyal to the Northern cause, transferring her activities to Washington. For a short period she labored as a nurse, and loved the job even though she disliked Dorothea Dix; probably for the only time in her life she was greeted entirely by praise. After the war she vigorously opposed the lenient Johnson reconstruction policy, going so far as to support the canard that the President had participated in the plot to assassinate Lincoln. Johnson's retaliation, getting her fired, is at least understandable.

In spite of her unhappy marital background and her deeply emotional nature and the usual sharpness of her observations, the views of Mrs. Swisshelm concerning the rights of women were surprisingly mild. Not only did she never coöperate with the leading feminists of her day, but she scoffed at their conventions, and felt that many of their ideas were silly; she gave only lukewarm support to the demand for suffrage. Typical was her reaction to the bloomer costume. She was open-minded and quite willing to try it out, but after experimenting for parts of two days decided it was ridiculous and only aroused laughter, and so she abandoned it permanently.

The only feminist reform that Mrs. Swisshelm was willing to admit needed immediate and positive action was the improvement of married women's legal rights; even here she felt that the change was already well under way. As to other conditions she felt that women had little cause for complaint and should certainly feel none when they compared themselves with Negro slaves. Where, she asked, was the law that prevented a woman from being the captain of a ship, or doing any other job in which she was interested and for which she had the proper ability? While a woman traditionally did not enter certain occupations, Mrs. Swisshelm scoffed at the idea that there was any male conspiracy to debar her. Just let her demonstrate her capacity and it would not be long before she was accepted. Such moderate arguments had considerable appeal, particularly when stated in the direct and effective Swisshelm prose, and they were disseminated quite widely, since most publications depended heavily on material clipped from other papers and since Mrs. Swisshelm was almost always quotable. The result was that the Swisshelm writings, largely in obscure Pittsburgh and St. Cloud papers, had much more influence than would have seemed likely.

The most attractive of the literary feminists was Elizabeth Oakes Smith, who combined personal beauty with literary success. Henry Clay, that connoisseur of feminine charm, quite properly praised her as "irresistibly fascinating." At the height of her powers she was tall and commanding, with regular features of a patrician cast. Her wavy brown hair and her brown eyes added to her beauty. She dressed carefully and fashionably, never adopting the bloomer costume. She spoke calmly and moderately but eloquently, and her voice was pleasant. Altogether, she was a lovely woman.

Mentally, Mrs. Smith was definitely superior, with not only high intelligence, but also with an unusually excellent memory and a high degree of sensitivity. Her mind was both keen and versatile. Everything seemed to interest her, from Egyptian history to prison reform. She gave attention to mountain climbing, birds, archeology, abolition, biography, diet, astronomy, French history, slavery, international politics, orphanages, and furniture, among other things, and her writings showed this breadth of interest.[12]

One of the most important of these interests, and one which she retained throughout life, was a deep concern with the occult. Even as a girl, Mrs. Smith felt that she had clairvoyant powers, could see at times when others found the light inadequate, could look into the human body to detect diseased organs, and could feel correct presentiments of the future, as of a bridge about to collapse.[13] She preserved carefully a "Psychometric Reading" of her personality by "Psycho-Magnetic Physicians" who gave "Clairvoyant Examinations" by having the doctor hold in his hand in a sealed envelope samples of the patient's handwriting. She attended séances and accepted their phenomena as authentic. Later in life she told how her twelve-year-old son had been burned severely at a Fourth of July celebration, and how she had put him asleep with "magnetic passes" so that when the doctor came he could bandage a sleeping boy. All through her life she referred frequently to spiritualism, which obviously fascinated her.

The beliefs of Mrs. Smith came more obviously from her youthful experiences than was the case with other feminists. Practically every one of them can be related immediately to personal events. Born and raised in Maine, at an early age she went through the trying experience of her father's dying and her mother's subsequent remarrying. Whether for this reason or another, Elizabeth had a nervous breakdown before

107

the age of six. Evidently of superior intelligence, as she grew a little older she developed the idea that she would like to teach awhile, and then live in the home of some Bowdoin professor so as to acquire a higher education by a sort of osmosis. Her mother pricked this iridescent bubble by insisting that no daughter of hers would ever become a schoolma'am. Any properly reared girl, according to her mother, got married and devoted her energies to a home of her own.

Elizabeth's dreams at the age of sixteen were no match for her mother's persistent realism. She was married. Her husband, Seba Smith, was in many ways a fine catch. He was a successful editor, and author of the famous Jack Downing letters, which had given him a national reputation. But to a teen-age girl he was far from a possible object of romantic affection. As she described him, "Mr. Smith was almost twice my age, wore spectacles, and was very bald."[14] While Elizabeth in the superficial sense was physically mature, she was still a growing girl and far from prepared psychologically for marriage. Seba Smith certainly deserves censure for marrying a girl half his age, no matter how attractive, but he also merits a bit of sympathy for having tried to please a very energetic wife who always thought of him as "Mr. Smith," and whose deeply religious idealism emphasized the goal of immaculate purity.

The marriage was successful as far as the outside world could see. Seba was a kindly and tolerant husband, and there were no bitter disagreements. Five children were born about as closely together as nature would permit. All of them were boys, and Elizabeth expressed pleasure that they would not have the troubles which they would have had if they had been girls. She also remarked rather casually that "Mr. Smith rather prefers boys,"[15] but did not indicate the practical effects, if any, of his preference.

Very unfortunately for the Smith family, Seba decided to sell his paper and devote his entire attention to writing. The writing turned out not so profitable as he had hoped, and when his major investment collapsed in 1837 the family, which now included four small children, was poverty-stricken. In this extremity the Smiths moved to New York, where they could become acquainted with the leading literary figures of the day, and where there was an easier access to publishers than in Maine.

Both Seba and Elizabeth turned their attention to writing, and curiously enough Elizabeth was more successful, winning high praise from no less a person than Edgar Allan Poe. She wrote everything from fairy tales for children to poetry and novels, not even disdaining letters to newspaper editors, and she preserved all her work carefully, as the large collection now in the New York Public Library attests. Her productions appeared in the newspapers, magazines, and gift books, and between board covers. Her long poem "The Sinless Child" was received very enthusiastically in the early '40's, although today it is considered quite bad. Her novel *Bald Eagle* was one of the best-selling of the Beadle series, while *The Newsboy* (1854), descriptive of New York life, went through twelve editions in its first year; it can possibly be described as early Horatio Alger, being the story of poor and honest Bob, who rose in the world through his pluck, with help through the discovery of the person who kidnapped a rich merchant's child.

Literary success brought lecture offers, and Mrs. Smith did a vast amount of speaking in the years 1851-64, part of it in lyceums. These lectures were on various subjects, but a good many of them concerned the position of women. They were well prepared and well delivered, and were given good notices even by newspapers that disagreed with their point of view. One small but significant index of the personal acceptability of Mrs. Smith was the invitation by P. T. Barnum for her to act as a judge in a baby contest he sponsored. While in one sense this was a small matter, and while she refused because she felt such exhibitions to be unseemly and ostentatious, the fact that she was invited by that superior judge of popularity, P. T. Barnum, had real meaning.

The latter part of Mrs. Smith's life was sad. Her husband became an invalid and died in 1868. Her popularity waned, and she had more difficulty in placing her writings, with payments declining. Speeches became less frequent in spite of appeals to friends and acquaintances for help in obtaining engagements. For a short time she was pastor of an independent church, and once she tried to sell encyclopedias, traveling as far west as Batavia, New York, but with little success. Moreover, she became more conservative in her opinions, feeling that the world was in bad shape and that the youthful generation was going to the dogs because of a lack of discipline. More and more her mind centered upon death, although unlike Mrs. Livermore she expressed no desire to hurry to a reunion with her husband. Her death came at the ripe age of eighty-seven, an impressive age for a woman who had complained of ill-health most of her life.

Mrs. Smith's feminism can be no surprise, either by its existence or by its exact contents. Her opinions came directly and recognizably from her personal experiences. They received most complete expression in her book *Woman and Her Needs* (1851), which appeared first in serial form in the *New York Tribune,* but were also stated in numerous other writings and in her speeches. Mrs. Smith was never particularly concerned with equal rights, although she did want certain legal restrictions removed. Her great plea was always for women's opportunity to develop their full capabilities.

Women, according to Mrs. Smith, were different from men in both bodies and minds, although she felt that physical sex was often overemphasized in view of the fact that "it has no part in the soul—it is not an essential ingredient in our humanity."[16] The outstanding qualities of women were beauty, flexibility, subtlety, love, compassion, and intuition;

intuition was much to be preferred over logic, which was more plodding and less trustworthy. Whereas a man was frequently cruel and selfish, a woman was usually unselfish and highly moral: "The angels recognize her as of near affinity."[17] These admirable qualities should be tapped for the good of society. If women voted, they could correct bad conditions over which they had had no control.

For personal development more opportunity was also desirable. "It is the making woman a creature of luxury—an object of sensuality—a vehicle for reproduction—or a thing of toil, each one, or all of these—that has caused half the miseries of the world."[18] Too many women have never developed their capacities properly, and have become discontented when their homes did not completely occupy their energies. Then also many girls married too young, when they were not properly prepared. Since no girl should marry until she is mature both physically and mentally, she should be trained to earn her living during the years before her marriage. Not only would the woman then be able to meet any possible emergency, but marriage itself would be greatly improved because the partners would be more equal. Then, with practically universal happiness in marriage, divorce could be prohibited. Most women would undoubtedly continue to marry and spend most of their lives in the home, but the golden ideal was a future world where women would develop their maximum capacities, associate with men on a basis of equality, and contribute their special and admirable qualities to the perfection of human society.

Elizabeth Oakes Smith was a very real asset for the feminists. Utterly charming as a person, she gave the lie to the usual canard about the soured old maid. Her considerable literary reputation gained attention for her when she talked about the position of women. The moderateness of her views, which included a large tincture of the traditional, made her more effective than the average feminist. All told, she was

111

an important force in advancing current changes in the position of women.

7
Professional Women

THE ACTIVE-MINDED WOMAN of the mid-nineteenth century found literature a socially acceptable outlet for her surplus energy, but a great many ambitious and intelligent women had no aptitude or ambition in this direction. Some of these women were sufficiently aggressive to push themselves into professions which had hitherto been monopolized by men, and under these circumstances a reasonable speculation would be that such professional activities and feminism would be natural corollaries. The energetic woman who defied social prejudices by insisting upon being a doctor or lawyer might be expected to have the kind of mind that would question the eternal validity of sexual divisions of occupation; she might feel bitter when such concepts limited and even frustrated her personal ambitions. This generalization, no matter how plausible, is difficult to support by convincing evidence. Certainly there were professional women with feministic leanings, but there were others who had traditional views on subjects other than their own particular work.

The profession most frequently adopted by women during the nineteenth century was teaching, although some question may be raised as to whether the word *profession* is properly descriptive, either by contemporary or by modern standards. If pay was a test of status, then current opinion placed teaching on a somewhat lower level of skill than work in a textile mill. Ordinarily no special training was required, and the teacher might be a college boy on his long winter vacation, or a young Miss waiting for Prince Charming. Since teaching was one of the few white-collar occupations open freely to women, it was rapidly becoming feminized, somewhat to the

113

distress of those who felt that the education of children should not be placed almost exclusively in the hands of unmarried women.

Teachers showed some evidence of feministic leanings. A large proportion of the women who later became outstanding feminists did at least a little teaching in their early lives, and almost inevitably resented the poor pay women received. This resentment was shared by thousands of other and nameless teachers, who peppered the pages of the educational journals with articles deploring the wage differential based upon sex. There is little evidence, however, that teaching frequently produced feminism, or even that the desire for higher wages indicated a generally feministic slant on life. Rather, the feminists did teaching, while other teachers had at least temporary objections to their low pay.

One of the best examples of the teacher-feminist was May Wright Sewall. May E. Wright (her maiden name) was born near Milwaukee into an intellectual family, with a father who taught, and was both a teacher and a feminist practically by inheritance. Apparently she was both bright and conscientious. Immediately following her schooling she started to teach, and she continued her pedagogy through and after two marriages, both of her husbands also being teachers. Her correspondence seems to show her as not wildly enthusiastic about "the little pests"[1] under her care, even though at times she proclaimed that she loved them. In fact she had periods of deep depression, caused in part by overwork and in part by the untimely deaths of her two husbands, whom she loved dearly. An an educator she was far from radical. While she believed in better education for girls, she held that the sexes should receive different kinds of education because of different qualities of mind.

Mrs. Sewall worked hard for suffrage for many years, but her main reputation came from organizing and managing women's clubs. Later in life she turned her attention mainly

114

to world peace, and was one of Henry Ford's guests on his peace ship the *Oscar II*. In her later life, after the death of her second husband, she increasingly turned toward spiritualism for consolation. While she was never an outstanding advocate of the largest opportunities for women, her general popularity was a real asset to the feminists.

The better-known women educators such as Catharine Beecher, Almira Phelps, and Emma Willard were far removed from feminism; in fact Miss Beecher argued strongly against the vote for women. Such women supported better education for girls and higher pay for women teachers, but here was the end of any hint of feminism. They generally accepted and reinforced the traditional division of activities between the sexes, trying only to make their students more effective along traditional lines. Most American schools followed the same pattern. Education was a method of transmitting traditional social patterns and not of reforming society.

The professions other than teaching and writing that were particularly interesting to women during the middle and late nineteenth century were religion, medicine, and law, all of which acquired their first female practitioners. One should not assume, however, that every woman minister, doctor, or lawyer was revolting against the commonly accepted place of women in society, and was therefore inevitably a feminist. An outstanding example of a non-feminist was Elizabeth Blackwell, the first woman to receive a regular medical degree. Miss Blackwell was radical only in the sense that she substituted medicine for marriage in her own life, and even here she was swimming with a strong popular tide of opinion that women would make desirable doctors within the limited area of treating women and children. She felt that women were superior to men in morals, but thought quite realistically that most women would get married and would be forced to make concessions to "the less spiritual and more imperious nature"[2] of their husbands. They should express the nobler

115

parts of their natures, but not often in the fields normally monopolized by men; in fact, Miss Blackwell made very caustic comments about women who stumped for suffrage. In general her point of view was conservative; she had no evident desire to change the relative position of men and women.

Women in the ministry were no historical novelty, going back at least as far as Biblical times, when women did prophesying and exhorting. Even in America there had been outstanding women like Anne Hutchinson, Jemima Wilkinson, and Mother Ann Lee, who had preached. Some of the smaller sects such as the Shakers gave women equality in the ministry, while the Quakers always permitted women to speak in meeting. Furthermore, the current idealism held that women were more moral and religious than men, kinder and more sympathetic, and generally closer to God, which should have made them highly eligible for the ministry but apparently did not. The Catholic Church of course excluded women completely from the ministry, then as now. The Protestant churches were almost equally hostile to the idea of female ministers, the great majority of Protestant pastors greeting with shocked horror the possibility of a break in the male monopoly. Women were confronted with a difficult struggle to gain even a toehold in the profession.

The first American woman to graduate from a recognized theological school and to occupy a pulpit as a regular minister was Antoinette Louisa Brown, a New York State girl. Unfortunately there exists little information about her early experiences except that she seems to have been extraordinarily religious. After a period in a girls' seminary she tried teaching for a time, and then continued her education at Oberlin, where she knew Lucy Stone. Just at what period of her life she became concerned with the place of women is uncertain. Later she protested that Oberlin girls were not allowed to debate or to read their graduation essays, but whether she objected to these limitations while she was in college is unknown.

116

After graduating from Oberlin in 1847, Miss Brown returned to register for the theological course. The consternation of the professors must have been great; at least, upon her graduation in 1850, the faculty refused to license, ordain, or encourage her. The result was the very difficult situation of a minister with no church. The Reverend Miss Brown filled her time by lecturing, but she found the life very difficult, particularly because, in her own words, she had "no self confidence." Her objective was to save enough money to take the time to write a book explaining why the Bible, in spite of the apparent meaning of its words, did not really advocate the subjection of women.[3]

Antoinette Brown's greatest splash of publicity came when she was a delegate to the world temperance convention at New York in 1853. An effort to stop the seating of women delegates was beaten, and the Reverend Miss Brown then took a place on the platform—presumably as a clerical prerogative—after which she advanced to the front of the platform to make a speech. Immediately pandemonium broke loose, with dozens of people trying to object to a speech by a woman, but with no one able to make himself entirely audible because of the general confusion. Among the disturbers were of course those favorable to the Reverend Miss Brown, and particularly Wendell Phillips, labeled by the *Times* as one of the "she-males" who supported "the female pests."[4] Ultimately the meeting voted that a woman should not sit upon the platform or speak except by special invitation, whereupon the chairman invited the Reverend Miss Brown to speak. Once more the noise rose in volume, and the speaker's voice was lost in the hubbub. Miss Brown stood on the platform for an hour and a half while the chairman ordered everyone into the gallery, and then asked the delegates to return to the floor individually as their names were called. Even this stratagem was unsuccessful, and Miss Brown finally left the hall without having delivered her speech. As a way of confirming women in their feminism, this sort of treatment was very effective.

Finally the Reverend Miss Brown was offered, and accepted, a pastorate at South Butler, New York. Her ministry proved very short, for in approximately a year she retired, giving her health as the reason. No doubt this explanation had some basis, but probably more important were her theological questionings. After much mental turmoil she moved from the Congregational to the Unitarian Church. Her promised return to the ministry was further delayed by the fact that she fell in love with Samuel Blackwell, a brother of Lucy Stone's husband, and married him early in 1856. After her marriage, Mrs. Blackwell continued to be known generally as the Reverend Antoinette Brown, even though she made no particular point of the matter. The fairly immediate results of the marriage were six children, which quite effectively limited Mrs. Blackwell's outside activities to periodic speeches. Apparently the speeches were not much better than in earlier years, for at least the kindly Mrs. Martha Wright thought one of them dull. Marriage, however, seemed to have at least one good effect on Antoinette Brown, improving her health and appearance; the *Times* in 1859 commented that she looked younger than ten years earlier.

Antoinette Brown's feminist views were not extreme. She agreed that men and women were not then equal in capacity, and felt sure that they would never be identical in feelings and beliefs. Furthermore, she criticized severely her own sex, holding that altogether too many women were cruel, unjust, untruthful, and slanderous. Her main plea was that women be given equality in education so that they could approach certain male standards and make their proper contributions to society. To the charge that women did not have sufficient physical strength for more education, she replied that as long as they could survive their restricting and uncomfortable clothes they could also survive better education. She argued that such education would open jobs freely to women. She insisted that every woman should learn a gainful occupation, and she foresaw the time when housework would be simplified, and much of it performed outside the home, so that women would have more time to follow their own inclinations. As to marriage, she wanted equality between husbands and wives and disapproved of divorce except for fraud.

Miss Brown's greatest contribution to the feminist cause was her attitude toward the Bible. She insisted that the Bible was not to be taken literally, and that if critical parts were interpreted correctly, they would prove not to portray women as inferior. Her importance was not in the novelty of her ideas, for others had said the same things, but in the added authority that came from having them said by a minister.

While Antoinette Brown was the first woman graduate of a theological school, Olympia Brown, who was not related to her, was the first woman to be ordained by a regularly constituted ecclesiastical body, and to have a considerable career in the ministry. Olympia Brown was unusual in being born in a log cabin in the relative wilderness of Michigan, and also for being influenced by her mother more than by her father. Apparently her mother was a forceful and iconoclastic person who impressed Olympia deeply with her ideas. The daughter was steeped in all sorts of reform proposals, including the desirability of a change in the position of women.

Olympia Brown's stimulating mental background inspired in her a desire to go to college, and when Olympia found the University of Michigan closed to women she traveled south to Antioch College. Several of the essays she wrote at Antioch have been preserved, and give some clue to her frame of mind at that time. One written in 1860 was entitled "Female Character" and made the general point, with a minimum of punctuation, that whether woman "be an instrument or ornament whether a fool or drudge or an angel the good of society & the well-being of the race demands for her the fullest mental

& moral development." While she believed in the possibilities of her sex, she showed at this time no evidence of being a flaming crusader for women's rights.[5]

Following Antioch, Olympia Brown attended the theological school of Lawrence University at Canton, New York, where she was admitted by the faculty with resignation as a Christian duty, but with no enthusiasm. Graduating in 1863, she was ordained to the Universalist ministry, and cared for several churches, at first in the East and then in Wisconsin. After meeting Susan B. Anthony in 1866 she became a more active feminist, and during the following year assisted in the losing effort to capture Kansas for suffrage. The Reverend Olympia Brown married a Wisconsin newspaperman in 1873, but continued to keep her maiden name. When her husband died twenty years later, she took over the management of his newspaper and printing business in Racine, Wisconsin.

The Reverend Olympia Brown was active in the agitation for women's rights, though never one of the best-known leaders. Her ideas, as expressed in her speeches and writings, quite naturally were rooted in Christian philosophy. She held that Jesus embodied within himself both masculine and feminine traits and that his church should consequently give equal treatment to men and women. She tended to downgrade men and upgrade women. For her, men were generally low and boorish, and their position of dominance was unfortunate: "Ours is an aristocracy of bifurcated garments, whose escutcheon is the moustache; whose insignia is the spittoon; whose palace of state is the smoking-car; whose Herald of approach is the curling tobacco smoke."[6] On the other hand, distinctive feminine traits—love, self-sacrifice, high morality, religious devotion, and love of justice—would benefit both the church and society as a whole if allowed free expression. The result of equality of the sexes would be a beautiful symmetry such as had been intended by God.[7]

Medicine was another profession to which women should

have been welcomed with open arms if people had recognized the proved capacities of the sex, or even if they had accepted the obvious implications of their own beliefs. Women had long practiced medicine. The farming wife was the custodian of herbs and other medicines, and treated almost all of the family's illnesses, even those which were fairly severe. Practically all childbirth, in either country or city, took place at home with only a midwife in attendance; a doctor was seldom called except for an exceptionally complicated case. Furthermore, the usual current ideology held that women by nature were angels of mercy, with special sympathy for the sick and an innate aptitude in their care, and with the necessary stamina to endure longer nursing stints than could the presumably stronger male. But in spite of both fact and theory, a long struggle was necessary before women were accepted as either nurses or doctors. As nurses, the feeling was that woman's modesty would and should make her unavailable. As doctors, modesty was also a factor, particularly in relation to male patients, while home duties were held to be a great deterrent, at least for a married woman. Practically everyone agreed that female characteristics would always debar women from surgery.

In spite of popular resistance, a few women began to practice medicine, although often as botanic doctors, hydropaths, or other irregular practitioners. They were not admitted to regular medical schools before mid-century, although the disadvantage of this exclusion was not so great as might be imagined. They were always excluded from local medical societies, which meant mainly that they could not use legal means to collect patients' debts. A changing public sentiment was evident at least by the 1830's, with an increasing feeling that women would be useful as doctors, particularly for the troubles of women and children, and by the early '50's several medical schools were established for women. And then, as

121

pressure increased, the regular men's schools gradually and reluctantly began to admit women.

The process of transition from irregular medical practice to a more normal situation was well exemplified in the experiences of Harriot Kezia Hunt, who has sometimes been called incorrectly the first American woman doctor. Harriot Hunt was born (1805) in Boston to an old and religious New England family. She was a first child, even though her parents had been married fourteen years, her mother being thirty-five. The birth was very difficult, and at first it was thought that the baby was dead. Little wonder that Harriot was the center of her parents' attention and was badly spoiled. After the birth of a second daughter, her mother divided her time between the two girls. But her father was even more important than her mother in Harriot's life. When he died, during her early adolescence, she wore mourning for six and a half years. In her autobiography she recorded: "I pined for my father: he was always ideal as well as real, to me."[8]

Harriot Hunt never married, and one can only speculate as to whether her celibacy was related to her adoration of her father. Her autobiography gives no hints of the usual love affairs of adolescence or of any later romantic attraction. On the other hand, there is no indication of a dislike for men unless one considers suspicious an almost morbid obsession with cases of seduction. Her most frequently expressed opinion of marriage was that it should not dominate a girl's early thoughts and that every girl should be trained to earn her own living.

As a pampered daughter, Harriot was sent to private rather than to public schools, and she found school work both enjoyable and easy. As always throughout her life, she was very religious; at this period her devotion was to John Murray and his Universalism, while later she was attracted to Swedenborgianism. After she finished her education she did some teaching, although she never thought of teaching as a life occupation.

The real turning point of Harriot Hunt's life came as a result of the serious illness of her sister, who was desperately sick for most of a year. Various doctors tried their laxative and bloodletting techniques, but with no advantage, and so the girls read some medical books and ultimately transferred their allegiance to an English couple who treated primarily the mind. The invalid recovered, whereupon the sisters worked awhile with the English couple and then set up practice for themselves, emphasizing psychotherapy. They wisely refused to take obstetric cases or to do surgery. Throughout a lifelong practice of medicine Miss Hunt remained convinced that much so-called disease was actually nonexistent and that many of women's real troubles were unnecessary, provided that women were given more and better physical training. To disseminate these ideas she lectured widely on physiology.

The medical practice of the Hunt sisters was disturbed by the marriage of the younger one, although at first the new husband moved to the young women's home, creating a sort of matriarchy, of which Harriot was the head. But in 1847 the sister and her husband established a home of their own, whereupon Harriot decided that she needed more professional training if she should continue to work by herself. As a good Bostonian she naturally thought first of the Harvard Medical School, and applied for admission. The startled faculty followed its first impulse and turned her down. Three years later she applied again, and by this time the professors had apparently become accustomed to the idea of a woman in their classes; at least they admitted her. But then the male students were embarrassed and raised such a ruckus that she was advised to withdraw, as she did. After another three years she was given an honorary M.D. degree by the Female Medical College at Philadelphia.

Dr. Hunt was by all accounts an attractive person and an excellent doctor. Everyone seemed to like the "little lady doctor"[9] and spoke particularly of her kindness, her cheerfulness, and her practical common sense. Her practice was large and lucrative, so that she could live in a spacious and well-decorated house. Apparently she continued through life to keep the rather unusual emphasis on the patient's mental attitude.

In addition to her practice, Dr. Hunt found time for many other activities. When the influential New England Woman's Club was formed, the organizational meeting was held in her home. She spoke rather frequently at woman's rights conventions and on the lecture platform. While she contended for general equality of men and women, her main emphasis was on the proper education of girls, including adequate physical training, and on increased legal rights for women.

Dr. Hunt appeared before the American public largely because of her yearly protest against paying taxes when she did not vote—taxation without representation. She growled that while even the most stupid and ignorant man had the suffrage, intelligent women were left unrepresented. Here, she said, was the reason that girls received poorer education than boys; they lacked the pressure of potential ballots. Quite significantly she did not go as far as Mrs. Stone and Mrs. Foster, and refuse to pay her taxes; her protest consisted of only a written statement expressing her point of view.[10] The conservative *New York Times* was impatient with Dr. Hunt's attitude, which it considered silly, and commented that what she really wanted was a law reading: " 'Be it enacted, that all women shall become men; this act to take effect immediately.' "[11] The obvious untruth of the charge is less important than its indication of one kind of opposition that women like Dr. Hunt had to meet. But in spite of such ill-tempered comments, normally Dr. Hunt was well received and did a great deal to advance the cause of women in medicine and the general status of all women.

More effective as a doctor but must less attractive as a woman was Mary Putnam Jacobi, who in many ways represented the younger and more adequately trained women doctors. Mary Putnam was the daughter of the well-known publisher George Palmer Putnam, an intelligent and tolerant man. He was quite willing to have his daughter act as she thought proper, although at times he thought her too precipitate, and urged that she postpone decisions until she was quite certain of her desires.

Mary (commonly called "Minnie") had superior intelligence and an extraordinarily forceful personality. She tended to dominate the people who surrounded her and to be scornful of others with less ability and assurance. Her qualities were those which were commonly labeled masculine, and there is possibly some relation between this fact and her reluctance to change from girlhood to physical maturity; at the age of twelve she felt very unhappy about approaching maturation, and this frame of mind may well have been responsible for her dislike of the girls' school which she attended and her rebellion against her church, the Baptist. Later, as a married woman, she signed herself "M. Putnam Jacobi."

The general attitude of Minnie makes understandable her decision to embrace a scientific career, commonly considered the exclusive prerogative of men. Her father did not oppose her decision, although as usual he urged delay until she was quite sure; unfortunately he went bankrupt just before Minnie was fifteen and hence could not help his daughter financially as much as might have been expected. The most important part of Mary Putnam's educational career included study at a New York school of pharmacy, at the Female Medical College of Philadelphia, and in Paris as an honor student. On returning to America from Paris she taught at the Woman's Medical College of New York, but both the students and her boss, Dr. Elizabeth Blackwell, were unhappy. Dr. Putnam was extremely impatient with slower minds, which included almost everyone, and persistently talked over the heads of her students and gave them work beyond their powers. The latter part of her life was spent in an extensive private practice, in which she emphasized pathology and was considered particularly skillful in treating children's diseases.

Mary Putnam's three important love affairs were illuminating. All three were with Jewish men, by a coincidence at least remarkable. The first, which came before her medical career, was an unhappy experience. The family did not approve her choice, but this fact was of little importance as compared with the fluctuations of Mary's feelings. When she was with her fiancé she felt affectionate and even passionate, but this feeling changed rapidly to indifference when he was away, and in fact she was increasingly unhappy as her marriage day approached. She recognized that she had the much stronger personality and questioned whether her half-wifely, half-maternal feeling was a good basis for a happy marriage. At times the young man impressed her as childish, when she felt that he "should be my master and superior."[12] She was relieved when her father, realizing her frame of mind, terminated the engagement.

By the time of Mary's second affair, in Paris, she had apparently given up the impossible search for a man who would be her "master and superior." Since this episode terminated when the couple could not agree whether to live in France or America, perhaps the affections of neither party were deeply engaged. The third case involved a professionally suitable partner, the German-born Dr. Abraham Jacobi, president of the New York County Medical Society. The doctors were married and had three children, of whom two died in infancy. The Jacobis were both respected as physicians.

Dr. Mary Jacobi was first of all a physician, and secondarily a feminist—or even a woman. She had little sympathy for the contention that women were oppressed and enslaved, since, as she put it, who would "oppress the mother that gave him being, the wife that he invites to share his home and the daughter whose sweet devotion is the very sunshine of his life"?[13] Only in her later years did she give active support to suffrage for women. The point at which medicine and feminism coalesced in her mind was in the training of women for medical careers. She argued vigorously that even a girl of moderate mental endowment was competent to undertake the study of medicine and that a married woman doctor faced no insuperable difficulties in practicing her profession. As illustrative of this contention, Dr. Jacobi was herself a prime exhibit for the feminists, since she not only was a doctor with a fine reputation but also exemplified concretely that a childbearing wife could continue to practice medicine successfully. She recognized the difficulties of combining motherhood, medical practice, and research, but felt that possibly these very difficulties inspired greater achievement.

Most radical of the women doctors was Mary Edward Walker, a New York girl who acquired her ambition to be a doctor from her father. She received her M.D. from Syracuse Medical College in 1855, and after nearly starving in private practice, which apparently suffered mainly from the lack of people willing to experiment with a woman doctor, became an assistant surgeon in the Army during the Civil War. The latter part of her life she spent in private practice in Washington, D.C.

Dr. Walker, an ardent feminist, gave visible evidence of her frame of mind by wearing men's clothes from the time she was sixteen. During the war she adopted the same uniform as her fellow officers. In Washington her costume was a frock coat and striped pants during the day, and full evening dress for lectures and parties; her only concession to femininity was curly hair. She never married, and late in life established an "Adamless Eve" colony to provide an ideal environment for other spinsters. Some have thought that Dr. Walker opened the way for women in army service, but more obvious were the hostility and ridicule that she inspired. She was probably more of a hindrance than an advantage to women in their struggle for more rights.

127

A possible nonmedical outlet for women interested in the health of their sex was to study a little physiology and then to lecture to women on the subject. Various such lecturers appeared on the American scene, and they usually felt that their work was a part of the more general effort to advance women's status. Two of them, Paulina Wright Davis and Mary Gove Nichols, attained particular eminence. Their only real similarities were in their lectures and in the fact that each had two husbands.

Paulina Kellogg, to use her maiden name, was an orphan from the age of seven, and reared in western New York by an aunt who was both very religious and a strict disciplinarian. Paulina accepted docilely her aunt's beliefs and dreamed of becoming a missionary, but her dreams were shelved when at the age of twenty (1833) she married a wealthy Utica merchant, Francis Wright. With the untimely death of her husband, Paulina was left with ample financial resources but no occupation—a situation deeply disturbing to a woman imbued with a high ambition to help others.

After much thought about her circumstances, and inspired by the writings of the eminent phrenologist George Combe, the young widow concluded that her best possible service would be to encourage women to understand their own bodies more thoroughly, and to treat them more considerately. Obtaining a chart of the human body, she started to give physiology lectures to women. She became so absorbed by her vocation that she did not allow her work to be greatly interrupted even by her marriage to Thomas Davis of Providence, Rhode Island. The result was that when her new husband went to Congress in 1853, he was a trifle embarrassed because many Washington residents looked askance at a female lecturer, particularly when she exhibited "unladylike" charts of the human body.

Mrs. Davis was drawn quite naturally into the feminist movement, becoming a partisan of Mrs. Stanton. Her own story of the origin of her feminism was that at the age of sixteen she had suddenly awakened to the narrow place occupied by women, but since her memory was not trustworthy, there is at least a possibility that the awakening came later and more slowly. In any case, however, she was active during the 1850's, appearing at many conventions, speaking frequently, and now and then presiding. Her greatest contribution, made possible by her personal wealth, was the establishment of a monthly feminist paper, the *Una,* at Providence in 1853. Later it moved to Boston. At its masthead were the words: "Out of the Great Heart of Nature We Seek Truth." While the *Una* lasted less than three years and was hardly exciting with its long essays and novels, its reports of conventions, and its letters to the editor, it was still a valuable asset to the cause of woman's rights.

Paulina Wright Davis was slight and fair, with gentle manners, and fitted the current description of "ladylike." She spoke infrequently and then in a voice so low that it was often inaudible. She was reported to be an affectionate wife, a good housekeeper, and a diligent needlewoman.[14] Her appearance of delicacy was justified by the fact, for most of her life was marked by ill-health, which probably explained at least in part her periodic fits of depression. From time to time she would make some such statement as "I have been and still am in deep affliction—My heart so torn that it has been hard for me to give a thought to the world."[15] Now and then during a period of depression she protested the tendency of her own sex to accept advantages won by others but to refrain from doing anything on their own behalf. Physical weakness may help also to explain the acceptance by Mrs. Davis of the reality of the phenomena of spiritualism. On one occasion she described how during a recent illness she had been attended by three doctors, but that "the spirit of my darling brother was my only physician," solely responsible for her recovery.[16]

The feministic activities of Paulina Wright Davis were the

manifestations of a deeply emotional and religious nature, but they were also an outlet for the restless mind of a woman sufficiently wealthy not to need gainful employment. She herself noted that feminist activities produced happiness by giving her a feeling of importance and of value to the world. Her emotional nature found deep satisfaction in work which she felt had vital social advantages.

The ideas of Paulina Wright Davis were those of most of her co-workers, and reflected neither disturbing personal experiences nor great depths of thought. Men and women were different, but such differences implied no inferiority. The size and strength of men carried no implication of superiority any more than was implied by the size of rank weeds which crush delicate flowers. Ample evidence existed from the past that women had great potential abilities, and while many women were far from perfect, the sex should have an equal chance to show its inherent talents. Mrs. Davis was troubled about how women were to obtain increased opportunities for employment, and debated seriously with herself whether it was proper for them to take the jobs of male strikers.

Present-day marriage, according to Mrs. Davis, is legalized prostitution, giving men a legal screen for the display of their gross sensual passions. Wives should be made equal in all matters, but particularly they should have control over their own bodies, including power to limit the number of their children. "We ask to be regarded, respected, and treated as human beings, of full age and natural abilities, as equal fellow sinners, and not as infants or beautiful angels, to whom the rules of civil and social justice do not apply."[17]

Mrs. Davis may have seemed radical to some Americans, but she was calm, moderate, and reasonable in comparison with another lecturer on female physiology, Mary Sargeant Neal Gove Nichols. The latter was born Mary Neal in New Hampshire, and her early life remains vague in spite of the multitudinous bits of self-revelation in her writings. Probably

130

her parents were somewhat iconoclastic, reading receptively
the radical literature of the day. Certainly they were not well-
to-do, and in consequence Mary had a limited education. She
is reported, although with doubtful documentation, to have
been avid for information and to have studied French, Latin,
and medicine by herself, to have written poetry for the newspapers, and to have taught district school. At the age of
twenty-one (1831) she married a New Hampshire boy, Hiram
Gove. The couple had one child. Now Mary started the study
of physiology in earnest, and when she and her husband moved
to Lynn, Massachusetts, she gave lectures to women on the
subject, both at Lynn and elsewhere.

This first marriage was never happy, and in 1840 Mrs.
Gove finally deserted her husband. By this time she had acquired an interest in a remarkably comprehensive list of reforms, including vegetarianism, mesmerism, Fourierism, temperance, rational dress, and spiritualism. In 1844 she appeared
in New York as a water-cure physician, and two years later
published her *Lectures to Women on Anatomy and Physiology*. After the usual description of anatomy and of bodily
functions, together with the usual good advice on proper food,
drink, and clothes, she came to her main objective, to sell the
idea of the water-cure. Her central theme was that *"all curable
diseases can be cured by water,"*[18] and that while water was
particularly good for the specials ills of women, it was also
successful with such varied ailments as burns, scarlet fever,
deafness, and lockjaw; in fact its only limit seemed to be broken
bones. Water was used in wet sheets and bandages, vapor
baths, and foot and other baths. It was to be absorbed through
every available opening in the body. In her time, water-cures
had considerable popularity in the United States, and Mrs.
Gove carried her claims to the greatest possible extreme.

During 1847 Mary Gove met a real soul mate, Thomas
Low Nichols, not only akin to Mary in temperament and
beliefs but also a child of New Hampshire. Thomas had an

131

iconoclastic mind, an infinite capacity for adopting and fighting for reforms, and a roving foot. After a year at Dartmouth he had entered newspaper work, first in New York City and then as editor of the *Buffalonian*. His columns were too vigorous for the taste of some of the local residents, with whose disapproval the court agreed, so that Thomas was convicted of libel and jailed. His distress seems to have been alleviated by letters and visits from many women, of whom some were married; he was always attractive to the opposite sex.[19]

At about the time that Thomas Nichols emerged from jail, he was well-nigh the universal reformer. Obviously he favored prison reform, and he also embraced such diverse paths to utopia as the elimination of liquor, tea, and coffee, the acceptance of mesmerism, and the adoption of women's rights. He could support the vegetarianism of Graham, the associationism of Fourier, the ideals of John H. Noyes as expressed at Oneida, and the individual sovereignty of Josiah Warren all at one and the same time. His union with Mary was a case of real affinity; Mary's ultimate divorce from her first husband and the marriage of the happy couple was a somewhat belated concession to the power of public opinion.

The activities of the Nicholses were amazingly varied and complex. After Thomas had spent a period at the New York University Medical School so that he could place an M.D. after his name, the couple advertised themselves in New York City as "Water Cure physicians." They edited a water-cure paper under the rather intimidating but all-embracing title of *Nichols' Journal of Health, Water-Cure, and Human Progress.* Soon they became restless and moved to Cincinnati, shortening the name of their house organ to *Nichols' Monthly.* During the years 1856 and 1857 they conducted a water-cure establishment at Yellow Springs, Ohio. In addition they spoke widely and wrote extensively. Among the writings of Thomas was an *Esoteric Anthropology,* which treated the "most intimate relations of men and women." Mary's productions, in addition to her *Lectures to Women,* included an autobiography and *Woman, in all Ages and Nations.* Together, they published *Marriage, Its History, Character, and Results.* Ultimately the Nicholses were converted to Catholicism, and presented the remarkable spectacle of people who believed in Catholicism and spiritualism at the same time. With the coming of the Civil War they felt so unhappy in the United States that they moved to England, where they spent the rest of their lives.

The views of Mr. and Mrs. Nichols were so similar and so interwoven as to be impossible to disentangle. The Nicholses agreed in general with the philosophy of Josiah Warren, who has been called the first American anarchist, and claimed as a good friend Warren's best-known disciple Stephen Pearl Andrews, who wrote an introduction for one of Mrs. Nichols' books. The basic concept was complete personal freedom for everyone, both male and female. With this ideal accepted, the machinery of trade was to disappear, as were courts, judges, lawyers, and politicians, with the result that undesirable human traits would be replaced with the desirable traits which would be permitted expression in this utopian world.

An obvious part of the future free world was freedom for women, but the Nicholses were little interested in such mundane matters as employment, education, and politics. Domestic slavery was to end, with love following the untrammeled dictates of the heart, with children only if desired, and with machinery to do most of the work of women. The Nicholses' obsession was with the personal relations between men and women, and here they spoke with such startling frankness that many people considered their books pornographic. The existing marriage institution, according to the Nicholses, was highly immoral, providing a legal cover for husband and wife to exploit each other, with no more freedom than a brothel. The partners should be equally free to enter or to leave the union at any time, and in fact a certain amount of variety was desirable; the Nicholses asked rhetorically

133

whether you would be satisfied always to smell the same rose, no matter how pleasant the odor. With true love the partners were really married, regardless of the attitude of church and state; without love, there was no marriage. In simpler and more generally understood language, they said at other times that what they advocated was the elimination of marriage.

The Nicholses spent large amounts of space in detailing their concepts of the attitude of women toward sex and marriage. They held that many marriages were contracted to permit sexual satisfaction, but then confused the issue by holding that most women "never feel the sexual desire as a controlling motive,"[20] and that in fact most women never feel the urge at all. They argued that a woman should have the right to pick the father of her children, and then asserted that, because so many women had neither sexual nor maternal urge, with real freedom for women the birth rate would drop 90 per cent.

Quite obviously the Nicholses could hardly have been the idols of more moderate feminists. To a woman such as Mrs. Paulina Davis, Mrs. Nichols was a distressing creature who wore impossible clothes and held deplorable views. Most feminists were glad to sweep the Nicholses under the rug and try to forget them. For the considerable part of the United States that viewed feminism with open hostility, the Nicholses were fine examples of the extremes to which people were certain that feministic doctrines inevitably led.

Law was a profession that opened very slowly to women. Lawyers, including judges, were no doubt conservative in their social attitudes, but much more important was the conviction of the general public that women had no aptitude for legal reasoning and court arguments. This attitude was widespread not only in the mid-nineteenth century but also in the mid-twentieth century, and among both men and women.

Whether or not women were generally unfitted for the practice of the law, there were certainly a few members of the sex who felt otherwise, and who gradually pushed open the doors of opportunity. Iowa was the first state to admit women to practice—Mrs. Arabella A. Mansfield in 1869—and then other states followed suit. Many lawyers of the mid-nineteenth century were trained entirely in private offices, but gradually the law schools attained precedence. The first law school to give a degree to a woman was Union College at Chicago (Ada Kepler in 1869), and other schools followed in a very deliberate procession.

Apparently some of the early women lawyers entered the profession largely by accident. Mrs. Laura DeForce Gordon, first woman to be admitted to the California bar, had been married and divorced and had worked in journalism for some years before her attention turned to law. Mrs. Myra Bradwell, first woman to be admitted to the Illinois bar, and then an early practitioner before the United States Supreme Court, first studied law as a way of helping her husband in the editing of a law review. Both Mrs. Gordon and Mrs. Bradwell worked actively for woman suffrage, which was entirely natural in view of their personal difficulties as women and their particular interest in the processes of government.

Possibly most interesting of the early women lawyers was Mrs. Belva Lockwood, the first woman to be admitted to practice before the United States Supreme Court. She was born in New York State (1830), and at the age of eighteen married a farmer, by whom she had one child. Her potentially commonplace life was completely disorganized by the untimely death of her husband, and she was left with the task of providing for the support of herself and her child. The obvious outlet was teaching, and for the next few years she taught at various places, with a few interludes to obtain further education. As an intelligent woman she noticed the relatively poor pay of the female educators and also the general social implications of this disparity, just as had Susan Anthony, who also knew teaching from first-hand experience.

After the Civil War Belva McNall (she was not yet Lockwood) opened a school in Washington, D.C. Here it was that she met and married the successful dentist, Dr. Ezekiel Lockwood, who died in 1877; her luck with husbands was poor. In later years Mrs. Lockwood said that she entered the law because it paid better than teaching, but this explanation is certainly too simple, since she undertook her legal training while her husband was still alive and amply able to take care of her. She graduated from a Washington law school in 1873, at the age of forty-three. Her successful legal work concerned particularly claims against the federal government, and it was in this connection that she found admission to the Supreme Court desirable. When her first application was refused she embarked on a Congressional lobbying campaign which eventuated in the necessary legislation. Her actual admission took place in 1879.

Mrs. Lockwood was an ardent feminist. Mrs. Stanton quoted her as advising unmarried women not to marry, and married women not to sew on buttons and rock cradles until they were given the vote.[21] Because of this well-known aggressiveness and her eminence as a lawyer, in 1884 and 1888 Mrs. Lockwood was a natural candidate for the Presidency under the banner of the Woman's National Equal Rights Party of California. She received a few thousand votes, but there is no evidence that the major parties were seriously concerned by, or even aware of, the threat of this new rival.

The slowness with which women entered law and other professions was due much less to legal disabilities than to the effects of popular pressure, as Mrs. Lockwood herself pointed out very clearly.[22] She contended that the real bar to the entrance of women into the professions was public opinion. Her argument was that women were sensitive and hated to be laughed at if they departed from usual occupations, and that above all they feared that any such iconoclasm might lose them the admiration of men. According to Mrs. Lockwood, the future opportunity for women depended above all on the willingness of women to make the necessary effort.

8
Mavericks

MOST FEMINISTS can be grouped according to their backgrounds and interests, but a few failed to fit any neat pattern. They went their own unique ways, unwilling to make the concessions and compromises necessary for coöperation with others. For them, it was the others who should make the adjustments. They were the mavericks of the woman's rights movement.

The feminist who theoretically deserved the greatest sympathy, and who actually received the least, was Eliza Farnham. Eliza's early life was so tragic that it practically made normality impossible. Born in Rensselaersville, New York (1815), she lost her mother before she was six and was reared by a drunken uncle and a frowsy, bad-tempered, nagging aunt. The only way in which the motherless, unhappy little girl could remove herself from her unpleasant surroundings was to withdraw into the realm of her imagination, trying to ignore her foster parents. She admired her father from a distance, and longed for the love and tenderness that she did not receive in her daily life. She thought of herself as ugly, awkward, and unattractive, and hence was shy and unsure of herself, with almost no friends of her own age. She was not sent to school until she was fourteen, and then because of her uncultured home was forced to find her reading in long accounts of Congressional debates, reports of the Secretary of the Treasury, and similar pieces of light fiction. A considerable outlet for the lonely little girl was dreams of great feats of valor which she might some day perform, and at the age of twenty she tried to realize at least a part of her hopes by traveling to Illinois. The results were disappointing, although she must

137

have had something of a thrill when she published an account of her experiences. Upon her return she married a lawyer, Thomas Jefferson Farnham, by whom she had three sons. When he died in 1848, she soon married William Fitzpatrick, by whom she had a child who died in infancy. In spite of her second marriage she retained the name of Farnham.

While Mrs. Farnham felt an unconquerable urge to express herself in numerous books, she wrote nothing about her husbands, which leads to the speculation that her marriages were far from being absorbing and satisfying emotional experiences. A further bit of evidence is her embarkment upon a personal career at the very time she presumably was taking care of a husband and small children. During the years 1844-48 she was matron of the women's section of Sing Sing, where reputedly she was successful by emphasizing kindness rather than severity. She then spent a short time in the Boston School for the Blind, after which she was attracted by the Gold Rush of 1849 and tried to collect a party of women to migrate to California. Failing to lure others, she made the trip by herself. Then, after the inevitable book on her experiences, she studied medicine in New York. Starting in 1859, she arranged successfully the migration of several groups of women to California. Her death occurred in 1864.

Mrs. Farnham spoke and wrote extensively but ineffectively. Her lectures were badly organized and poorly expressed, were dull and monotonous in delivery, and were further made unattractive by the speaker's poor personal appearance, since she was "a masculine looking woman,"[1] tall, spare, and angular. Her books were likewise badly organized and phrased, possibly in part because of her lack of education. They give the impression of a desperate but failing effort to express some deep emotional urge. Undoubtedly they were the products of an overwhelming desire to explain, at least to herself, a confused personal psychology which she did not understand.

Mrs. Farnham claimed that her views on women were

acquired about 1842, which would mean several years after her first marriage, and which in turn would suggest some connection between her marital experiences and her feministic views. The truth of this speculation is very doubtful. Mrs. Farnham was highly introspective and somewhat unstable emotionally. Her recollections are open to question. It is at least as possible that her views about women came out of childhood speculations as that they came from her marriage. Certain of them, as expressed in her writings, were impossible until Darwin published his views (1859).

The thinking of Eliza Farnham was concerned little with the educational, economic, and political rights of women. Nor did she speculate about the possible equality of women and men, for she was absolutely sure that women were superior to men, both physically and mentally. Women, she held, were much more highly developed in the evolutionary sense than men. Men resembled the lower brutes in their hairy awkwardness, while women had no facial hair and exhibited much more beauty and grace than the other sex. Among other indications of female evolutionary superiority was the fact that women had fully developed breasts, while men had only rudimentary and undeveloped breasts; incidentally, she here advanced a theory opposite to that presented by Darwin.

"Life is exalted," wrote Mrs. Farnham, "in proportion to its Organic and Functional Complexity," and since the feminine nature is more complex and all inclusive, woman's "position in the scale of Life is the most exalted—the Sovereign one."[2] Women have three periods involving different sexual characteristics, though men have only two, but most important, woman posseses the superior "Maternal System," involving parturition and lactation. Mrs. Farnham felt that the male part of reproduction involves no more than the feeding of the ovum and that all hereditary traits in children come from the mother. Any similarity of the child to the father is no more than the result of the mother's thinking.

139

Women, agreed Mrs. Farnham, have lesser physical strength and smaller cranial capacity than men, but she minimized the importance of physical strength, and held that the smaller feminine brain is more quick in understanding and more delicate in perception, while the female nervous system is more finely developed. Men are more acquisitive and egotistic; this fact and their greater strength make them superior as soldiers, mechanics, and pioneers. Women are superior in purity and morals, tact, and love of mankind, and have higher spiritual power. If women are bad, the badness comes from the influence of men. The great superiority of women derives from their maternal power, and after the menopause this entire potentiality is channeled away from the physical into the mental, which means that later in life women can make their greatest contributions to the community—sympathy, peace, philanthropy, love, and piety.

The inferior position of women in the past has been the result of insensitive men's using their greater physical strength, but even in the past men recognized subconsciously the superiority of women. Men reverence their wives and mothers for their purity and influence. Painters, poets, novelists, and sculptors idealized women and pictured their finer traits. The failure of women to shine more in the pages of history was due to the world's great concern with war and diplomacy, and also to man's inability to understand the more complicated feminine nature. "Woman is a mystery to man by transcending both his consciousness and his capacity for experiences."[3] The central point was that "woman produces and includes man,"[4] which means that while the all-including woman can easily understand any man, the woman is beyond man's comprehension. But the future promises that women's superiority will be recognized. Then will arrive "the Era of spiritual rule and movement,"[5] when pure women will exercise their rightful superiority over simple-minded and selfish men.

Almost equally convinced of the natural superiority of

women was Isabella Beecher Hooker, one of the remarkable children of the great New England divine, Lyman Beecher. While Isabella was a small girl, her father moved to Cincinnati to head a theological school devoted to the recovery of the great West from the Devil, the Pope, and Joe Smith—or at least that is the way he analyzed the situation. After Isabella had spent some time in the school of her sister Catharine, her mother died, and so in 1835, at the age of thirteen, she was sent to the school of her sister Mary in Hartford, Connecticut. She grew up to be an attractive young woman, and at the age of nineteen married a promising law student, John Hooker. The Hookers made their home in Connecticut their entire lives, mostly in Hartford. They had four children. John became a well-known lawyer, but in spite of his conservative profession was always something of a reformer. He helped establish the community at Nook Farm, and it is reported that he intensified his wife's feminism by reading Blackstone to her. The views of husband and wife were in fairly close agreement on practically every subject.

Isabella Hooker was an impressive woman. Her superior family and educational background gave her reputation, poise, and a great fund of knowledge. In appearance she was tall and slender, well dressed, keen-eyed, and beautifully mannered. Olympia Brown considered her the most charming and attractive woman she had ever met. Mrs. Hooker had full realization of her admirable traits, and in consequence exhibited tremendous self-assurance, sometimes interpreted by others as arrogance and self-righteousness. Apparently she never questioned the correctness of her views, or her ability to take charge of any situation that confronted her. She wrote extensively, and the perusal of her writings is a really noteworthy experience. She never used a single word where a sentence was possible, a single sentence when a paragraph could be developed, or a simple statement when she could think of a shower of tense adjectives that would make the meaning

141

obscure. She was very proud of her speaking, even though many auditors were not equally impressed. On one occasion she was so pleased by a speech she had prepared that when the meeting for which it was planned had to be canceled, she preserved her work carefully for twelve years until a proper opportunity was presented for its delivery.

Men and women were created equal, according to Isabella Hooker, who brushed aside impatiently the words of St. Paul, but women were actually superior to men in such vitally important characteristics as piety and morality. Women's highest function was maternity, and while at one time the strong arms of men were necessary for the protection of women and children, now the strong arms were giving way in importance to the strong brains, possessed by women. What women most needed was legal and political power so that they could protect themselves and their children.

The main consideration in the relations between men and women was sex, and Mrs. Hooker's thoughts reverted continually to this subject. The basic problem came from the fact that women were "feebly endowed with this passion," while men were "overstocked";[6] the one modification of this generalization was that women were less ardent in part because of their fear of pregnancies, and she suggested the "safe period" as a partial answer. Mrs. Hooker was no believer in the glories of physical sex and was concerned above all in reducing the amount of its expression. She favored frank sex instruction for children and advised mothers to spend particular attention in teaching their boys self-restraint; the exact nature of the instruction was left unstated. Prostitution was to be eliminated; certainly not to be tolerated and regulated by the state. She held that the participants quite properly should be subject to "its natural and God-ordained punishment,"[7] which sounded very much as though she approved of venereal disease as a deterrent to sex expression.

Marriage, according to Mrs. Hooker, was marked by "the

unreasoning and inordinate indulgence of animal passion on the part of the man, and affectionate submission on the part of the woman."[8] The main reason why base, brutal, and cruel men opposed the ballot for women was that they were afraid it would bring restrictions on their sensual indulgences. The proper goal for women was to refuse to satisfy the lusts of men, and in consequence to rise to their high destiny as the spiritual leaders of the race.

Mrs. Hooker's writings give the definite impression that she was morbid on the subject of sex. The natural deduction is that presumably she tended to be frigid and hence deprecated male passion. This deduction seems doubtful, however, because of the fact that her husband had identical views and because there is such great difficulty in visualizing John Hooker as an excessively demanding husband. Whatever the origins of Mrs. Hooker's feelings, clearly she placed heavy emphasis on the physical manifestations of sex as the basis for the most pressing problems and difficulties of women. She urged that in their meetings women's rights advocates devote themselves to the consideration of sexual problems, and was deterred only by the tact and firmness of Mrs. Stanton. While Mrs. Stanton was in rough accord with the Hooker views, she was more practical in tactics, and realized that flaunting the sex issue would be the very worst advertisement for women's rights.

The relations between Mrs. Hooker and Mrs. Stanton were far from idyllic. Mrs. Hooker never liked either Mrs. Stanton or Miss Anthony very much; her preferences went to Paulina Davis and Anna Dickinson. Her passionately held convictions, sometimes called unreasonable prejudices, when combined with her well-known lack of tact, antagonized Mrs. Stanton, even though Mrs. Stanton continued to write to her as "Dear friend." Miss Anthony asserted philosophically: "I resurrected Mrs. Hooker's letter & returned it to her with the nicest word I could say—on *mundane*—not ethical affairs— Well—we must take our fate—being so *'of the earth earthy.'*"[9]

After the feminist split of 1869 Mrs. Hooker expressed complete willingness to take over the NWSA and obtain a reunion of the two groups. Martha Wright referred deprecatingly to an eager and optimistic beaver, while Mrs. Stanton muttered about "the Beecher conceit,"[10] even though she then expressed her willingness to step aside for the good of the cause. When the Hookers became spiritualists, Mrs. Stanton wrote belittlingly of the "vague ideas floating in Mrs. Hooker's head."[11]

The involvement of her brother Henry Ward Beecher with "Lib" Tilton, together with the consequent suit by Theodore Tilton for damages for the alienation of his wife's affections, quite naturally was a heavy blow to Mrs. Hooker, at the time in England. She could not dismiss the charges completely, because they had first been made by her friend Victoria Woodhull, whom she admired very much. On the other hand, she could hardly place heavy blame on a member of her own immediate family, and so she came to the remarkable conclusion that "he was demoralized by that poor wife of his."[12] Possibly it may be said that here, as elsewhere, Mrs. Hooker's emotions took precedence over her intellect.

Mrs. Hooker's liking for the spectacular and questionable Victoria should not be construed as necessarily an indication of a lack of intelligence, for there were many other feminists of like mind. They included not only the radically minded Mrs. Stanton, but also such normally level-headed women as Martha Wright and Susan Anthony, who also expressed great enthusiasm. In fact it seemed for a time as though Mrs. Woodhull might dominate the entire feminist movement. Her rapid rise to power and her equally rapid fall—all in less than a decade—were among the more spectacular incidents in the quest for women's rights.

Victoria Woodhull's background was extremely uncertain except in the characteristic of undesirability. Her parents were unstable, unusual, and apparently not very much interested in their children. Her father was suspected of arson, while her mother was a mesmerist and spiritualist. One brother claimed to be able to cure cancer. Victoria herself saw visions even when she was a small girl. Her most usual ghostly visitor was a grave, tunic-clad figure who finally proved able to write his name in English as Demosthenes, thereby raising a trifle the curtain on Victoria's future. Vicky was married at the age of fifteen to a Dr. Channing Woodhull, whose profession of telling fortunes and selling an elixir of life inspires the suspicion that his medical degree was self-bestowed. The couple had two children. Possibly the fact that Victoria continued to call herself Mrs. Woodhull in spite of various marital vicissitudes may have indicated affection for her first husband.

The career of Victoria Woodhull emerged into the light of history when she and a younger sister, Tennessee Celeste Claflin, appeared in New York in 1868. The Claflin sisters, generally known as Vicky and Tennie, really set the city agog. Their patron was no less a person than Commodore Cornelius Vanderbilt, who had a deep interest in the occult, which was amazing in view of his hard-headed and shrewd business activities; while he was an elderly man, he was certainly far from senile. Backed by the Vanderbilt money, the sisters established an office at 44 Wall Street. Over the door they placed the sign: "Woodhull, Claflin & Co., Bankers & Brokers." When asked as to their competence, they contended that they had been properly informed by their father, whom they described as a wealthy merchant before he went bankrupt. Whether or not they did any banking and brokerage remains vague.

Not only did the brokerage business startle New Yorkers, but Mrs. Grundy found plenty of other material as the sisters opened their own house and went where they pleased without chaperon or escort. There were many raised eyebrows and scandalized whispers as it was noted that the ladies had a considerable succession of male visitors, who often arrived and left at questionable hours, while some of them apparently lived in the house, at least for a time. Particularly striking was a

145

dashing figure going by the name of Colonel Blood, possibly married to Victoria. The word "possibly" is used advisedly, since the amatory adventures of the sisters have never been disentangled.

The sisters replied vigorously to their critics, holding that as free individuals they had the right to order their own lives as they pleased. Vicky wrote: "I have an inalienable, constitutional, and natural right to love whom I may, to love as long or as short a period as I can, to change that love every day if I please!"[13] Very possibly this statement was actually prepared by a friend, Stephen Pearl Andrews, also a friend of Mrs. Nichols and the best-known contemporary advocate of free love. But in any case the sisters believed these sentiments, although it was rumored that Vicky was more vigorous in speech than in action, while Tennie was more promiscuous physically.

The Woodhull-Claflin views of sex morality were the culmination of much thinking about women and sex and marriage. Men and women should be as equal as nature permitted, and certainly women should have equal civil and political rights, which would improve the political life of the nation because of the superior morality of women. Every girl should learn an occupation so that she could earn her own living, which would at least permit her to be more particular in choosing a mate. More than this, however, as Tennie pointed out, with more industrial production work was leaving the home, and a day would come when residential areas would consist of many large hotels, with the wives practically freed from housework and customarily holding outside jobs.[14]

The sisters were bitter against existing marriage practices, holding that many girls were practically sold to the highest bidders, and that most women earned their livings by pandering to male passions, either inside or outside of marriage. With the goal of marriage, girls were trained only to catch husbands, even if the lure had to be artificial—for instance, padded hips and bosom, corsets, and cosmetics. The Woodhull-

Claflin ideas about premarital relations were unique. Such extramarital relations were accepted as both frequent and desirable, provided only that the woman were sufficiently wise to give the man not only physical gratification but also the spiritual uplift that he desired and needed. Women were held to be the seducers at least as often as men, and possibly men should be protected from predatory females, rather than the other way around. In every respect, the Claflin sisters wanted equality, with the elimination of the double standard of morals by sanctioning the same female as male actions. As for marriage, they preferred to abolish it, letting the permanence of any union depend on the continuance of affection. Furthermore they approved birth control and eugenics, looking with particular approbation on the practices of John Humphrey Noyes.

These extreme views, quite surprisingly, did not cause the sisters to be outlawed. They were extremely attractive and convincing. Victoria was tall, slender, curly-headed, and good-looking; she dressed simply and in good taste, and when anyone looked into her candid gray eyes he found it practically impossible to question her truth and sincerity. Her public speaking was equally effective, and she made a favorable impression when she testified before a committee of Congress. Her speeches tended to have a tinge of the erotic, which did not decrease their attractiveness. Theodore Tilton wrote that she was "one of the sincerest, most reverent, and divinely-gifted of human souls."[15] In case it should be pointed out that Tilton was a close friend, and possibly something more than a friend, similar statements can be quoted from others, such as Mrs. Stanton, Miss Anthony, and Mrs. Wright. For example, Mrs. Wright commented: "None can be with her without believing in her goodness and purity."[16]

The feminist leaders who had been so strongly attracted to Mrs. Woodhull naturally heard many of the innuendos about her private life. They sprang vigorously to her defense. Mrs.

Stanton, who shared some of the Woodhull views, wrote emotionally of the "sacredness in individual experience" and insisted that any criticism should at least not come from the women: "If Victoria Woodhull must be crucified, let men drive the spikes & plait the crown of thorns."[17] When Ben Butler, a long-time supporter of votes for women, questioned Susan B. Anthony about the Woodhull background, she replied tartly: "No, I have never enquired—neither have I about *yours*—it is a matter I have no concern with."[18] The tartness was no doubt due in part to the fact that Miss Anthony never quite trusted Butler; the reference to Butler's past was a very effective point.

The urge of both Vicky and Tennie toward self-expression led them to establish in 1870 *Woodhull & Claflin's Weekly,* a sort of house organ for the propagation of the views of the sisters. Soon there were rumors that the real purpose of the sheet was something less admirable—blackmail. Stories both then and later held that the main profit for the paper came not from printing, but from not printing, stories which various people found worth the cost of suppression. The most famous story that the *Weekly* printed concerned a presumed love affair between America's most popular minister, Henry Ward Beecher, and the wife of his friend, parishioner, and protégé, Theodore Tilton. Various explanations have been advanced for the publication, including the near bankruptcy of the *Weekly* and Victoria's desire to help her friend Theodore, but just as plausible is the protestation of Woodhull and Claflin that their action represented an attack on hypocrisy. The sisters asserted that they quite approved of Henry and Lib's following the dictates of their hearts, but they protested strongly that the Reverend Mr. Beecher should have been honest in his statements and not have castigated the sisters for the same actions in which he himself had indulged. Whether or not the charge was true may still be argued. The strongest evidence in its

148

favor is Lib's confession, but that statement was considerably weakened by her admission that she was a chronic liar.

The publication of this article set off a wild flurry of gossip in New York. Rumors, charges, and countercharges filled the air. Each side had its strong partisans. Anthony Comstock, the self-appointed guardian of American morals, seized the press of the *Weekly* on the charge of pornography, but ultimately failed to make the charge stick and had to return the press, whereupon the Claflins reprinted the article. The Reverend Mr. Beecher naturally denied the accusations, and was exonerated by several church investigations that changed no one's opinion. He threatened to sue for defamation of character, but never actually carried the case to court; incidentally, his wife supported him throughout the trouble. Tilton actually brought suit for alienation of affections, and the trial was the prime news story of its day. Beecher was not convicted, but the verdict of a divided jury did not carry overwhelming proof of his innocence. Rather surprisingly, Tilton seemed more badly affected by the incident than Beecher; ultimately his life came to an end in Paris, where he was sick, poverty-stricken, and alone. Beecher faced his detractors with courage and with his golden tongue, and ultimately was reinstated as America's most popular minister.

The Beecher-Tilton case produced all sorts of troubles for the feminists. The Stone-Blackwell group had long since warned Mrs. Stanton against associating with Mrs. Woodhull, but that fact was little consolation in the situation in which they found themselves. They perforce defended Beecher, who had long been prominent in their organization. The *Woman's Journal* talked of "The Tilton-Woodhull Conspiracy" as an effort by the advocates of free love "to destroy the reputation of an estimable lady and an eminent Christian minister,"[19] but was obviously unhappy about the whole affair, and kept its coverage at a minimum. The Stanton-Anthony people were in even hotter water. They necessarily supported the Tilton

149

side of the controversy, and both Mrs. Stanton and Miss Anthony consulted with and advised the Tiltons. But they came to realize belatedly and sadly that Tilton was not everything one could hope and that Mrs. Woodhull was a positive liability. Altogether too many Americans believed that Mrs. Woodhull was personally immoral and that she was running a paper devoted to pornography, to blackmail, or to both.

Even before the Beecher-Tilton trial, the relations between Mrs. Woodhull and the Stanton-Anthony people had been badly strained. Mrs. Woodhull was no shrinking violet, but thought of herself as the most important woman of her day. What more natural than that she should take over the NWSA and throw it behind her efforts to win the Presidency of the United States in 1872? First she had herself nominated by her own little group, but then hit a snag when Frederick Douglass refused her overtures to accept the second place on the ticket. When she moved to capture a convention of the NWSA, the scales had dropped from Miss Anthony's eyes and she foiled this particular coup by having the lights of the hall extinguished. Once Miss Anthony became aware of the real situation, she worked on her friend Mrs. Stanton, and the end of Mrs. Woodhull's influence was a matter of only a short time.

After Mrs. Woodhull lost her place in the feminist movement, she turned to lecturing. Her favorite subject was "The Garden of Eden," and she drew elaborate parallels between the Garden of Eden as described in the Bible and the organs and functions of the human body. Before many years both she and Tennie married well-to-do Englishmen and settled down to comfortable lives in England. In spite of their free-love theories they adopted rigorously monogamic habits. If sin invariably leads to degradation and sorrow, the sisters were extremely pure. If, on the other hand, the good die young, emphasis should be placed on the fact that Tennie lived to the age of seventy-seven, and Vicky to eighty-eight.

Any list of the eminent feminists of the nineteenth century

must include the name of Anna Dickinson, who was hailed in her day as the greatest orator of her sex. Unfortunately for her permanent fame her ideas were neither original nor distinctive, and her oratory was too flowery and emotional to appeal to modern ears. Her greatest service today is to provide a study in unusual psychology.[20]

Anna Dickinson was born to a Quaker family in Philadelphia in 1842. Her father, a merchant and an active Abolitionist, went bankrupt and died when Anna was two, leaving a family of five children, of whom Anna was the youngest. As a child, Anna was mentally precocious and an omnivorous reader, but at the same time an unattractive brat. While she was never pretty, she was spoiled as the baby of the family, and took full advantage of that fact. If she wanted her own way, the obvious method was to weep. She was opinionated, stubborn, and a fighter. Her temper was uncertain, with rapid fluctuations between periods of ebullient energy and optimism and fits of morose petulance. Her education was attained at a Friends' School. In religion, she found the Quakers too quiet for her taste and when she was fourteen moved to the Methodist Church, although she continued to wear the Quaker dress and to hold many Quaker ideas.

The earning of a living was a real problem for Anna Dickinson. The obvious possibility of teaching did not appeal to her because she resented the higher pay given to men. In spite of this aversion she taught for some time, although apparently she was a poor teacher. Then she tried other jobs, but her real talent emerged when she experimented with public speaking. Effective even at the outset, her power increased rapidly with practice. Soon she could devote her entire time to oratory—largely on abolition, temperance, and women's rights. Not only could she make a good living, but the public adulation was very flattering to her considerable ego; bearing on this point, her favorite art was a bust of Napoleon. During the Civil War she worked for a short time in the Washington mint. When she was discharged she attributed her dismissal to the fact that she was a woman and an Abolitionist, but others pointed out that her public charging of General McClellan with treason had at least a part in the decision to dispense with her services.

Both during and after the Civil War Miss Dickinson did a great deal of lecturing, at which she was fantastically successful. She appeared in practically every sizable town in the nation, and for some ten years her earnings ran over $20,000 a year, which permitted her to live in very considerable luxury. A good many of her speeches were political, and for most of her life she was a Republican, although she disliked Grant heartily and spoke for Greeley in 1872. In addition, she talked mainly of women's rights, temperance, and prostitution.

Success did not make Anna Dickinson happy, nor did it free her from anxiety. She was generous and extravagant, and was in periodic financial difficulties in spite of her large earnings. More important, she suffered from recurrent depressions, during which she feared that her fame was transitory. To maintain her status she embarked on all sorts of enterprises— wrote a couple of novels, acted as the star in a play which she had written, composed an autobiography, and even started to depict male stage roles with a characterization of Hamlet. These efforts were all unsuccessful, and it was at least clear that Miss Dickinson had no talent for writing or acting. In addition, the ventures were a considerable drain on her finances. To add to her unhappiness and further deplete her strength she squabbled with almost everyone in sight, including her lyceum representatives. At times she was so depressed that she went to the extreme of considering marriage as a solution. Among the men with whom her name was linked were the politician Ben Butler and the journalist Whitelaw Reid; for years she engaged in a lengthy series of quarrels and reconciliations with the latter. How seriously Miss Dickinson considered a possible marriage is an open question. Her excellent biographer concludes that she never was really interested because "she enjoyed the life of a heroine too much."[21]

There may be questions about the balance of Anna Dickinson's mind during most of her life, but there can be no doubt that it really tottered during her menopause. Among her unusual actions were lying on the floor and kicking her feet, having a dressmaker pull her fingers as a cure for a headache, raising her dress to show a visitor the scar of an operation. Rumors circulated that she had taken to drink. She was sure that people were plotting against her, and on this assumption quarreled with her sister, to whom she had been very close for many years, gathered her possessions in her bedroom, locked the door, and refused to eat or to wash. At last the insane asylum was called, and the attendants had to break down her door. At the asylum she protested vigorously that she was being badly mistreated and that her detention was a plot by her sister. Somewhat surprisingly the courts listened to her plea and freed her, although it took two trials to achieve this result. Upon attaining her freedom she initiated a long series of court actions against the newspapers for defaming her character; in a few cases she collected.

Anna Dickinson can of course not be cited as an example of the typical state of mind of a feminist, and yet it may be argued that her tremendous drive for recognition and power was merely an exaggeration of a similar feeling which others possessed in a less expanded and undesirable form. As to her contributions to the cause of women's rights, they were considerable. While she presented no distinctive ideas, and while she never would work satisfactorily in the various women's organizations, her speaking effectiveness should not be underrated. Countless thousands of Americans heard her, were favorably impressed, and henceforth had greater sympathy for the goal of expanded rights for women.

9
Changing Emphasis

FEMINISTS OF THE MID-NINETEENTH CENTURY placed their main emphasis on the winning of legal and political rights. Their more important organizations, which continued into the twentieth century, were devoted almost exclusively to attaining the suffrage. While the women were concerned with increased opportunities in every phase of life, they were convinced that a single and limited objective was desirable tactically, and that the suffrage would prove the key which would unlock every door, and ultimately make women free.

The earlier feminist leaders talked emotionally but only rather vaguely of the desirability of women's being trained to earn their own livings, and had little pertinent information as to the actual jobs which women held or might hold, even though they made some efforts in this direction. When they talked of education for jobs they tended to think of colleges and the professions. This frame of mind was quite understandable in terms of the backgrounds of most of the feminists, but was increasingly inadequate in a rapidly changing world where industry was pushing agriculture from the center of the stage, where commercial production was daily making housework lighter, and where more and more women were gainfully employed both before and after marriage.

Gradually there arose a new group of women more concerned with economic than political rights. Their attitude had been foreshadowed by Susan B. Anthony, Elizabeth Cady Stanton, and others who had stated that economic advance was the real basis for feminine independence, even though these women had in fact confined their work largely to the political sphere. Now as the nineteenth century approached its end, more and more women began to argue that if women would get proper job training, more employment opportunities, and higher pay, all other rights, including the political, would follow. This emphasis on the central importance of economic factors was in accord with the thinking of most contemporary liberals.

The changing emphasis of many feminists can be shown concretely in the attitudes of three well-known leaders. Caroline Dall, who pioneered in the heavy emphasis she gave job opportunities, devoted much effort to a detailed and moderately factual study of the work women were actually doing. Charlotte Gilman wove the economic emphasis into an elaborate philosophy which made her the ideal of many of the more liberal feminists. Rheta Dorr exemplified the attitude of the twentieth century as it was influenced by the Muckrakers. Even more important for the study of leading feminists, all three women had personal backgrounds that were unusual and fascinating.

Caroline Dall was born Caroline Healy in Boston in 1822. Her father was a well-to-do merchant and banker, and was glad to provide his daughter with tutors and private schools. Caroline's girlhood, with its comfortable home and fine education, should have been a happy one, but actually Caroline complained continually of illness, and longed for the affection and love that she felt she did not receive. She was certain that the only people who admired her were people she did not like, and that her own inability to give outward indications of affection cut her off from the usual close friendships. She even wrote pleadingly to her mother, begging for love and affection. Her unhappiness was so apparent that her schoolmates, with the usual insensitivity and even cruelty of youth, nicknamed her "The Disappointed."

Caroline always thought of herself as unattractive and hence avoided the boys and had no apparent adolescent love affairs. She commented that, since no one ever described her as feminine and since she could not bear to be called masculine, she must consider herself neuter. She refused to dance with the Harvard boys because she thought of herself as about as graceful as a duck. Niagara Falls appealed to her not as a honeymoon location but as a place where a girl might study theology with profit. When a fortune teller prophesied that she would be loyal to her first love, she agreed, because she held that her first love was the justice and kindness of God. Such sentiments involved a downgrading of men, whom she considered insufficient in reverence. Women were superior to men, and she announced that wives should rule their husbands with stronger hands, since "never was a horse so stupid that he could not appreciate a good horsewoman."[1]

The emotional nature of Caroline Healy, which felt itself frustrated in the normal outlets of family and friends, found expression in religion. Later, Caroline remembered questioning the authority of the Scriptures at the age of nine, and contended that her qualms "threw me back upon my own resources and made me at a very early age reserved, mistrusting, sad."[2] Possibly she confused cause and effect. For a time she considered spiritualism, but found it unsatisfactory, and reverted to her original faith in beauty, truth, and God, with close emotional ties to Jesus. She wept over Paley's *Evidences of Christianity*—seemingly a difficult feat. She felt a deep sense of guilt when she missed church. She loved teaching her Sunday School class, and when she left home some of her longest and most affectionate letters were to the girls of the class. She rapturized over Christian miracles, and devoted her life to obeying what she considered the call of duty.

The inability to make friends and the tendency to withdraw from normal activities did not imply any lack of self-confidence or any difficulty in making decisions. Caroline herself stated that "I have never known what it was to be *without* an opinion of *my* own."[3] She had utter confidence in her

157

ability to choose right over wrong, and was very generous in giving other people the advantage of her clear thinking. She said later that she never asked an opinion from anyone else, but always told others, including her mother and father, the right answers. Moreover, she felt that her thoughts and conclusions were of great and permanent importance, and even as a girl wrote them down at considerable length. When she was accused of conceit, she reacted with a feeling of injured innocence, since she was sure that she was only telling the truth, no matter how unpalatable to others. She saved all her correspondence, including her own letters, which she copied in letter books; eventually she gave some of her correspondence to the Massachusetts Historical Society for the benefit of posterity.

The relations of Caroline with her father were extremely important, but since our knowledge of them comes almost entirely from the daughter's statements, and since Caroline emotionalized all her experiences and interpreted them to justify herself, some caution must be used. Her memory reported that because of her mother's illness, her father was more than usually attentive to her while she was a small girl, and that she adored him. Not long after her religious questionings, and one is tempted to guess not long after her disillusion with Santa Claus, her eyes were opened at the age of ten to defects in her previously perfect father. Apparently her father's greatest flaw was that he did not always accept the judgments of his daughter; her statement was that "he refused to accede to many of the philosophical positions which I assumed."[4] While the great virtues of these "philosophical positions" of the ten-year-old girl have been lost to the history of philosophy and can therefore not be evaluated, there certainly developed an increasing coolness between father and daughter, Caroline being deeply hurt by what she considered a lack of proper appreciation and encouragement. She insisted that she always tried very hard to please her father, but obviously that effort did not include any willingness to accept his judgment. After all, she was certain that she was correct, and could hardly be expected to abandon truth for falsehood even to please him.

A vital change occurred in Caroline Healy's life when her father experienced business difficulties and went bankrupt. While Caroline felt sad that this turn of affairs "interfered with my metaphysical interests,"[5] she rose heroically to the occasion by announcing that she no longer was going to give way to sickness, and that she would enter the profession of teaching to help the family finances. She obtained a job near Washington, D.C., and for the first time left home, which was now idealized in her mind by a severe case of homesickness. Any girl would have found difficulty in adjusting to the new life, but Caroline was particularly lacking in adaptability; Southerners, too, had some natural doubts about a Boston Unitarian. Miss Healy was horrified by the institution of slavery, being particularly concerned with the effects on the whites, and much worried over miscegenation. She was strongly antislavery, but did not become an active Abolitionist.

During her stay in the South, Caroline Healy had her deepest emotional experience when she fell in love with a young Unitarian divine, Charles Dall. A lifetime of isolation from the usual human emotions made her reluctant at first to respond to his advances, and she explained this slowness by pleading a rather nebulous former love affair from which she had not recovered, the objections of her father, and the need to help with her sister's education. But soon the floodgates of her long-dammed passions broke, and she flooded her beloved with words of affection. She wrote to "dearest Charlie" in this fashion: "God bless thee, my own—and keep thee strong and pure—such as I may love never *too* well—never too anxiously—God bless thee."[6] She was sufficiently honest to inform Charles that her ideals were very high and that she was the managing type.

Charles and Caroline were married, but the union soon experienced difficulties. Caroline had the difficult combination of smouldering, subterranean passion and ideals of purity and chastity, while very possibly Charles had similar mental conflicts. Caroline's self-righteousness and her unconquerable tendency to tell others how to run their lives must have been at least trying. At any rate Charles seized an opportunity to work in Toronto, leaving his wife and children at home; Caroline's main reaction was to protest bitterly and continually the inadequacy of the funds he sent her. The Toronto experience ended in such a questionable financial tangle that Mrs. Dall's conscience later ordered her to repay some of the money. Charles turned over a new leaf by greeting enthusiastically a chance to do missionary work in Calcutta. Again he apparently was glad to leave his wife and children at home.

The Dall marriage rapidly became vague and dreamlike. The exact bases of the estrangement were later related in detail by Mrs. Dall to her son, but the pertinent three pages were then cut out of the letter book. Communications between Caroline and Charles became fewer and fewer. Letters from Charles are notably absent from the Dall correspondence, even though his wife had the instincts of a magpie; either he did not write or she destroyed his letters. Her communications became increasingly formal, except that on at least one occasion she tried "to cut to his heart—if he has any."[7] At times the couple transmitted messages to each other through a third party. On Charles' infrequent visits to the United States, husband and wife treated each other as little more than casual acquaintances, and Charles was so anxious to return to Calcutta that he was willing to go without pay.

Lacking a husband, and with two children to support, Mrs. Dall again retreated into her girlhood world of loneliness and isolation. She was sure that no one loved her, even her own family and that of her husband, and wailed that she "stood alone as few women ever do."[8] She tried to earn her living by giving speeches on women, and appealed to friends and acquaintances to find her engagements. These lectures were not impressive. She was not attractive personally, and read her remarks in a poor voice that tended to be inaudible. She then collected her speeches into books, of which by far the best-known was *The College, the Market, and the Court: or, Woman's Relation to Education, Politics, and Law* (1867). She was very proud of these publications, sending copies to individuals and institutions who she thought might benefit, and saving their polite notes of thanks. In addition, she wrote numerous magazine articles, having an almost complete mental collapse when one of them was refused.

Mrs. Dall never could coöperate well with others. She felt called upon to give advice to everyone about everything, whether asked or not, and thought of herself as particularly qualified in moral and religious matters, for she considered herself a minister of the Gospel even though not ordained. She realized that people did not always react well to the truth she revealed to them, but excused "my positiveness and my self esteem" by emphasizing her truthfulness.[9] Susan Anthony used the words "self conceit" and apparently was not so much impressed by the value of truthfulness.[10] The result was that Mrs. Dall was no bosom pal of other feminists and not very active in the women's organizations, even though she now and then appeared at the meetings. In fact Mrs. Dall tended to quarrel with other people, including numerous merchants with whom she did business and the members of her own family, and had a particularly violent and long-drawn-out struggle with her sister over the disposal of her father's estate.

Mrs. Dall's difficult disposition may have been in part a product of her precarious health, although it is at least equally possible that the disposition produced the ill-health. She wrote almost continually of how bad she felt and how her physical distress interrupted her speaking and writing. Periodically she held that she was upon the point of death, and on such an occasion might beseech her friends to republish her famous book after she had passed to her reward. She must have surprised both herself and others when she lived to the age of ninety, a remarkable age for a chronic invalid.

Mrs. Dall's thinking had an unusual emphasis on the employment of women rather than on the winning of the ballot, even though she agreed that women should vote and that their votes would improve political life. She collected much information about the legal disabilities of women, and was concerned about educational opportunities, holding that women should receive as much education as their abilities permitted, but above all she felt that women's money-earning activities were the core of the problem of improving women's rights.

Women of her day were ill-equipped for expanded job opportunities, argued Mrs. Dall. They were all too often frivolous and extravagant and indeed utterly useless. They were altogether too adaptable, seeking too frequently to please men, who wanted to maintain their male dominance by influencing women to deck themselves in frills and furbelows and to live in idleness. The current ideal of parasitism had not existed in the past and need not continue in the future. Historically, women had done a great share of the hard and dirty work of the world, though men had largely eliminated them from history. Even today they did a surprising number of things capably—more than most people realized—and Mrs. Dall listed such occupations as medicine, pharmacy, farming, business, and gymnastics in which at least a few women had demonstrated competence. Women had the ability to perform many jobs traditionally closed to them.

The scarcity of the jobs open to women had produced heavy concentration in a few industrial areas, and that concentration had meant lower pay, which in turn had led women into prostitution, for "lust is a better paymaster than the mill-owner or the tailor, and economy never yet shook hands with crime."[11] Certainly anyone would agree, said Mrs. Dall, that women would be at least as competent as men in such jobs as selling ribbons or sorting colors in floss, but men still monopolized these fields. In fact men protested vigorously if women entered such trades as printing, and these objections must be overcome to permit women to develop their potential abilities.

The expansion of job opportunities for women, with its accompaniment of higher pay, was largely in the hands of women themselves. They should be more self-reliant and independent. Particularly should outstanding women show more respect for labor, and be willing to take the lead in demonstrating that point of view to the world by themselves working.

The result of more women's working would be entirely admirable. For women who otherwise lived in idleness, life would become meaningful, since "disease, depression, moral idiocy, or inertia, follow on an idle life."[12] A wider choice of occupations and higher pay would be a godsend to women who had to earn their own livings. Unhappy marriages would decline and prostitution disappear as women were able to earn satisfactory incomes. Slowly business practices would become less immoral as women added their higher ethical standards. Moreover, "if women worked more, men might work less, and time for culture could be afforded to all."[13] Above all, men and women would become equal, with the result of a new, beautiful, and happier world.

Mrs. Charlotte Perkins Stetson Gilman expressed the contemporary economic emphasis in terms of the ideas developed by Edward Bellamy in his utopian novel *Looking Backward,* and of those of the anthropology and sociology of Lester F. Ward. Though her work was highly derivative, it had elaborations of its own, and altogether presented a complete philosophy that appealed strongly to many of the more advanced feministic leaders of the day.

The ideas which Charlotte Perkins (her maiden name) found attractive presumably had some relation to her early experiences, which were quite extraordinary. She was a great

163

granddaughter of Lyman Beecher, and if heredity has any importance, was well endowed with ability; certainly no one has ever called her stupid. Her parents were very much in love, but still separated when Charlotte was a very small girl. Her mother had three babies very fast, and when her doctor warned her that a fourth might be fatal, her father solved the problem by leaving home. His wife continued in love with him, but gave him a divorce so that he might marry again, which he never did; presumably he also continued to be in love, even though he found himself either unable or unwilling to contribute to the expenses of the family. The result was that, since Charlotte's father was not available while she was a girl, she was raised by a strict and poverty-stricken mother, whose destitution forced her to move her home about once a year. A corollary was that Charlotte received a relatively meager education.

The lack of material and educational advantages led Charlotte to a good deal of daydreaming, but she also read widely, for she was eager for self-improvement. Her rather indiscriminate reading gave special attention to such diverse subjects as elocution, calisthenics, and physics. One of her interests was religion, and she followed her mother into Swedenborgianism for a time, but ultimately discarded the occult, thought of God primarily as power or force, and accepted the doctrine of social evolution. Possibly her greatest discovery was that printed pages are not always correct; this conclusion came from finding an incorrect answer in a mathematics book.

This introspective and somewhat lonely life made Charlotte self-centered and self-righteous. She gave little consideration to others, and was so confident of her own conclusions that she boasted that for a period of eight years she did nothing wrong. Her emphasis on strength and self-reliance included a passionate desire to have a strong body; she was deeply convinced that she was not going to be a weak, sickly, dependent female. She refused to wear a corset, took much exercise, and could claim great strength and no illness. She was not inaccurate when she said at the age of seventeen that she was different from other girls.

Realizing that she had to earn her own living, Charlotte picked commercial art as her profession. After a period at the Rhode Island School of Design she engaged in teaching art and in doing commercial work, particularly advertising cards. Her life was completely disorganized when she fell in love with the artist Charles Walter Stetson. He was the most important man she had ever met, their interests were similar, and he was in love with her, but in spite of these attractions she valued her independence jealously and held off for two years before she said "yes."

Charles and Charlotte were married in May 1884 and started housekeeping in three large second-floor rooms. They were completely devoted to each other, and Charlotte found great pleasure in learning to cook. Soon she became pregnant, and discovered sadly that in spite of her former body-building program and her presumed resistance to illness, she felt worse and worse until Charles had to take over most of the housework. One can only speculate as to the importance of her mother's child-bearing experiences in this connection.

Charles and Charlotte hoped and expected that when the baby was born Charlotte would recover her health, but the advent of Katharine Beecher Stetson brought no such result. Even nursing the baby proved painful, and Charlotte spent most of her time lying on the sofa and crying. Something had to be done, and so Charlotte went to California by herself. As long as she was in California she felt fine, but as soon as she returned she collapsed and took to her bed. Life under such circumstances was impossible, and after many long and earnest conversations the couple agreed to separate, although with "unbroken mutual affection."[14]

After the separation, Charlotte spent a short time at home and then took her daughter to Pasadena, where she rested, and experimented with writing poetry, novels, and plays. Charles visited her, but they decided that a revival of their marital relations was impossible, and a divorce was obtained in 1894; later, Charles remarried happily. While Charlotte's health improved, there were periods of depression and collapse. She said that her mind was weak, by which she meant that she could neither read nor write for any extensive period, and that she was troubled by forgetfulness and indecision; on one occasion she said that she stood on a street corner for fifteen minutes trying to make up her mind to take a streetcar. These difficulties showed later in her writings, which she did in short, intensive spurts, with little preparation by reading and almost no revision.

Since living on a nonexistent income from writing was impossible, Mrs. Stetson moved to Oakland, where she ran a boarding house. Her spare time was spent writing, and in speaking on feminism. She was very sensitive, writing complainingly to Brander Matthews to ask his advice as to what she could do about Ambrose Bierce and his insinuations when she had no husband or brother to punch him in the nose. Her first published book was *In This Our World* (1893). These events were of minor importance, however, in comparison with her reading of Edward Bellamy's *Looking Backward*. She was completely convinced by the book, subsequently spent much of her time in speaking and writing on "nationalism," and incorporated the Bellamy ideas in all her later writings. She became a socialist of the Bellamy pattern, and later joined the Fabians and worked for the cause of socialism. Still following her mentor, she rejected the Marxian dogmas and never joined the Socialist Party of America.

The dominance of the Bellamy ideas appeared most distinctly in Mrs. Stetson's most famous book, *Women and Economics* (1898). She said later in her autobiography that the manuscript accepted by her publisher was written in seventeen days spent visiting five different houses, and in fact this pro-

166

duction, like others by her, shows evidence of hasty composition. She also said that in preparing for the writing she had read only two pertinent compositions, a book on the evolution of sex and an article by Lester Frank Ward in the *Forum*. This statement is obviously inaccurate, if for no other reason than her great dependence on Bellamy. The book was extremely popular with many feminists of the day, and Mrs. Blatch, daughter of Mrs. Stanton, wrote that it became "the Bible of the student body" at Vassar. This claim undoubtedly exaggerates the universality of Mrs. Blatch's and her friends' ideas, but still the book was an important and influential landmark in the development of feminist thinking.

The central theme of *Women and Economics* was that the traditional sex division of jobs was highly undesirable and that the future would see women take their proper place in the world. In the past, said Mrs. Stetson, women had been driven to depend entirely too much on the exploitation of sex. In this connection, Mrs. Stetson had written elsewhere of a young lady's saying that the purpose of a girl in social life "is to get a fellow so he cannot keep his hands off of you—and then not let him touch you."[15] Even after marriage a woman still depended upon selling sex as a way of life; she was pitifully dependent upon her husband, and she was paid on the basis of her husband's income and generosity rather than on the value of her services. The main difficulty was that women were confined to the home, whereas "all the varied activities of economic production and distribution, all our arts and industries, crafts and trades, all our growth in science, discovery, government, religion . . . are, or should be, common to both sexes."[16]

The road to improvement was to permit women to participate equally in all affairs outside the home. By this means women would become fully developed and independent human beings rather than creatures of sex, and would make distinctive and valuable contributions to society. To attain this end, women must be freed of the hampering restrictions of household drudgery so that they can work outside the home, and this change can be accomplished by mechanizing and specializing such jobs as cleaning, washing, and cooking, just as has happened to other trades. The experts could do better and more efficient jobs, even in such individualized matters as cooking; after all, people go to restaurants from preference. In a congested city area, hotels may solve the problem, but in the suburbs the solution would be kitchenless houses connected by arcades, and with central eating rooms. Cleaning, laundry work, and even the care of small children would be socialized profitably, wives being freed to contribute directly to the outside world. Obviously the main outlines of such a plan came directly from Bellamy.

Later years saw Mrs. Stetson continuing to emphasize this same communal activity, particularly in regard to cooking: "As to the kitchen, that has no place in a model home."[17] Following the Bellamy model, Mrs. Stetson admitted that a family could eat at home if it preferred, with a Food Supply Company furnishing the comestibles through an underground connection, the food brought up on a dumb waiter, and the dirty dishes returned similarly; but she insisted that a common eating place was much to be preferred.

Even before Mrs. Stetson published her *Women and Economics* she had returned East (1895) to engage in speaking and writing. Her most exciting experience was the meeting with Lester F. Ward at a women's convention. She had already been impressed with Professor Ward's writings, and considered him "the greatest man I have ever known."[18] He was to dominate her later writing. Incidentally, she also met her second husband, George Houghton Gilman, whom she married in 1900. The marriage seemed of such little importance that she failed to mention it in her autobiography, in which she refers to "Houghton" infrequently and casually.

The book Mrs. Gilman felt was her most important effort was *Human Work* (1904), although she admitted that it was poorly written. It did not sell well, which actually was a reasonable public reaction to a dull book. Mrs. Gilman felt, however, that her writings lacked popularity because they were becoming deeper and more philosophical. Her desire for a wider circulation of her views led her to establish a magazine of her own, *The Forerunner,* in 1909, for which she composed the entire contents. It lasted for seven years, by which time she felt that she had exhausted her ideas. Its tone may not be misinterpreted by quoting one poem which it contained:

The Ultra-Male

Said the Stallion to the Mare
   When she beat him on the course,
"It isn't right! It isn't fair!
   You're not a Horse!

"You are a Mare—not made for speed;
   You've no head, legs nor tail:
You're only meant to breed—to breed!
   To be a horse is Male!

"Don't try to make a Horse of yourself!"[19]

The central theme of *The Forerunner* was that in the past the female had always been at least equal to the male, and sometimes superior, while in the present world the pattern had been destroyed; the future would be improved if women regained their importance, and particularly if motherhood were given greater recognition and respect. Here was the theme of a long series of articles with the general title "Our Androcentric Culture, or the Man-Made World"; the word *androcentric* was taken from Ward. These articles were published as a book in 1911, and quite intelligently the title was abbreviated to *The Man-Made World*. Appropriately, it was dedicated to Lester F. Ward, "one of the world's great men," and author of the Gynaecocentric Theory, about which Mrs. Gilman announced that "nothing so important to women has ever been given to the world." The Ward theory, which Mrs. Gilman used as the foundation of her exposition, was that women were the superior sex, that they had developed the first industry and art, but that men had then used their superior strength to appropriate women's advances, to confine women to the home, and to remove from the home all occupations except those involving the worst drudgery; in the future, women would again come into their own in a gynandrocratic state where the sexes would be equal.

Mrs. Gilman spent much of her new book in detailing the badness of a world dominated by male passion, contentiousness, and egotism. The double standard of morals was a male invention, which left the man free to be immoral, while if the girl makes even one small slip "she has lost her market value and is thrown out of the shop."[20] Prostitution is an offshoot. The power of men to choose wives has reduced the beauty and health of women because men have preferred short-legged and delicate women whom they can dominate; the excessive illness of women comes partly from this situation and partly from women's confinement in the home. Fashionable clothes and elaborate ornamentation are symbols of feminine subserviency. The family is an absolute despotism operating in the midst of a presumed democracy, and women are slaves. Male dominance in the field of literature has eliminated women from history because men have confined themselves to praising male attributes of aggression and war. It has also brought the adventure story, which is distinctly masculine, and the love story which emphasizes the male obsession with sexual passion and which ends with marriage, thus omitting the more important mother love. Sports are usually masculine, emphasizing strenuous action and competition.

An emphasis on the woman's point of view would bring a vast improvement in world conditions, contended Mrs. Gilman, although she varied at times as to which feminine characteristics were inherent and inevitable, and which were the products of a male-dominated environment. As one small example, she held that women were unfitted for male sports because of their early training, while elsewhere she contended that present sports expressed distinctive male characteristics and would never be suitable for women. Through most of her argument, however, she contended that women were psychologically and emotionally different from men, and that these differences were an inescapable accompaniment of physical sex distinctions. "The sex instincts of the male are of a preliminary nature, leading merely to the union preceding parenthood. The sex instincts of the female cover a far larger field, spending themselves most fully in the lasting love, the ceaseless service, the ingenuity and courage of efficient motherhood."[21]

If the feminine ideals were brought into prominence, the world would improve vastly. The double standard of morals would be replaced by women's single and higher standard. "Society" in the undesirable sense of the term would be eliminated, with women exchanging the clinging draperies of subservience for more functional clothes and spending their time in productive work. Marriage would be improved as women picked better fathers for their children. Prostitution would disappear. Of course, married women would hold regular jobs outside the home, domestic industries being relegated to the archives of history. No longer would a woman doctor be forced to demonstrate her femininity by making strawberry jam, for people would recognize that desirable traits are not just "masculine," but rather common to both sexes; in fact the existing emphasis on sex is pathological and will be reduced to proper proportions in the ideal world of the future.

Other improvements would be practically unending. Education would be vitalized by eliminating rewards and punishments and substituting loving affection and coöperation. Ethics would become higher with the emphasis on love and religion. Sports would lose their stress on the violent and destructive, as exhibited in bullfights and prize fights. Literature would improve, with emphasis on books such as *David*

171

Harum and *Uncle Tom's Cabin,* although art might still remain the domain of the man. Government and laws would be simplified, with the introduction of real coöperative democracy to replace the current force exercised from the top. Crime would decline as loving care replaced punishment, and a better environment was provided. Maybe most important, war would be eliminated. "The male naturally fights, and naturally crows, triumphs over his rival and takes the prize—therefore was he made male. Maleness means war."[22] The substitution of female love and kindness for male aggressive competition would naturally eliminate war.

Mrs. Gilman talked at times of equality and coöperation between the sexes, but quite clearly her heart was elsewhere. Women were the superior sex. The ideal was not to add feminine traits to an essentially masculine civilization, or even to give equal rating to the two sets of standards, but for the feminine to replace the masculine. This result would come inevitably as women were freed from domestic duties, entered all phases of life, and demonstrated their superior ability and morals. The dream was for the masculine world to be converted into a feminine world.

Mrs. Gilman lived sufficiently long to see great expansion in the activities of women, and yet she was far from completely happy, particularly because of her rather prudish attitude toward sex. She had long insisted that sex was overemphasized because of male passions, and that its importance would decline as women became more important. She had held that in time men and women, like the lower animals, would confine their sex interests to one short period of each year and that the usual family would have no more than two or three children; she approved the small family and felt that its appearance by natural development obviated the need for birth-control measures save in a few exceptional cases.

By the 1920's, however, Mrs. Gilman observed that with more feminine equality men did not move toward the better female standards, but rather that female standards were moving toward the old, undesirable male concepts. She continued to bewail the "overdeveloped sex instinct," "sex-waste," and the apparent feeling that sex had just been discovered, but now she could hardly place all the blame on men. She had to change her explanation to emphasize general social pressure acting on both men and women: "Men and women are no more to blame for being oversexed than a prize hog for being overfat."[23] Mrs. Gilman continued to hope rather despairingly that sex would in time recede into what she felt was its proper and very small position in the world, but she had to admit that the current trend was in the opposite direction.

Rheta Childe Dorr was another woman whose point of view was greatly affected by her youthful experiences, and yet she did not permit these experiences to warp unduly her general appraisal of the world. Her particular contributions were her careful reporting and her effective presentation of the activities of women, particularly in the economic sphere. She devoted but little attention to ultimate goals and finely ramified philosophies, but saw the world in concrete and realistic terms.

Mrs. Dorr held that "feminism, like Boston, is a state of mind,"[24] and according to her autobiography obtained this frame of mind as quite a small girl, even though it was later reinforced by listening to Mrs. Stanton and Miss Anthony; in time she wrote a biography of Miss Anthony. While Rheta Childe was a none too happy girl because she irritated those around her by her persistent argumentativeness, by her unpredictable actions, and by her instant resentment of any suggestion of female inferiority, she still hated the idea of becoming a mature woman when adolescence came upon her. She attended the University of Nebraska, where in spite of her physical attractiveness, the same traits of pugnaciousness and resentment prevented her from becoming popular with either faculty or students.

After graduating from college Rheta Childe worked a

173

couple of years in a post office, and then went to New York to study art. A short experience convinced her that she would never become a successful artist, and she turned to writing. She thought of herself as a young woman of unusually strong sexual passions, and later she wrote: "I have little to say about my numerous love affairs or my long and insistent sex life."[25] Since many people overrate their sexual urges, since Rheta gave little evidence elsewhere of overwhelming physical desires, and since she apparently lost all interest in the matter before she was fifty, she may possibly have been doing a little unjustified boasting about the intensity of her passions while in her twenties.

Rheta Childe presumably solved her sex problems in 1892 when she married John Pixley Dorr. While he was twice her age he was vigorously masculine and well educated; best of all, he was eager to provide leisure for his wife to write. The couple settled in Seattle, and John spent much of his time in reading aloud from such classic authors as Spencer, Darwin, Carlyle, Diderot, and Hugo. The choice of Herbert Spencer proved to be a sad mistake, for ensuing arguments about the independence of women disclosed that John was unhappily conservative, whereupon Rheta searched for every radical opinion on the subject, and the discussions grew more and more heated. Both husband and wife became more and more immovable, and more and more irritated. Why, said John, don't you stop all this reading and theorizing and proceed with your supposed desire to write? To which Rheta flared angrily that she could hardly write effectively until she had seen more of life.

A possible reconciliation loomed when Rheta became pregnant, bringing her great joy, because she desired children. As usual her mind turned toward the acquisition of pertinent information, and so she read everything she could find on the subject of prenatal influence. She accepted the idea that the mother's mind had almost unlimited influence over an unborn child, and did everything possible to give a good start to her daughter—for she was determined to have a girl and not a boy. She always spoke of the coming child with a girl's name. She replaced all the decorations of the old-fashioned house with plaster busts of Greek goddesses and of Queen Victoria, she surrounded herself with beautiful flowers, and she spent her time making baby clothes even though she hated sewing. The actual birth was very difficult, but under the influence of opiates Rheta dreamed of herself as one of the millions of women who were the carriers of the race. Possibly anticlimactic was the fact that in spite of all this preparation the child turned out to be a boy.

The coming of the baby did not have the happy results that had been hoped. As soon as Rheta recovered her strength she spent all the time she could spare in roaming the streets and scraping acquaintance with odd characters who she felt would provide her story material, even though John was not convinced that this was the most desirable way to obtain life experience. When Rheta was at home she concentrated her attention on her son, leaving her husband to shift for himself. Hardly surprising was an increasing coldness between husband and wife. Soon they were sleeping in separate rooms, and then they decided to part completely, Rheta and her son going to New York (1898), where she planned to do newspaper and magazine work.

The early years in New York were not happy. While Mrs. Dorr had reasonable success with her writings, she resented bitterly the fact that she received less pay than men, and she found that living alone was difficult for a woman who considered herself highly sexed. Various men took her out, but they all assumed that she was the merry widow type, told her offcolor stories, and expected to be admitted immediately to her bed. Her answer was to go home alone and dream. For a period she says she almost became a man-hater, but then she was more and more fascinated by her work, and attained a better-balanced view of life. Possibly her experience shows that sex really can be sublimated.

Mrs. Dorr was mainly a reporter on the condition of women, particularly working women, and her writings appeared in the newspapers and in such magazines as *Everybody's, Hampton's,* and *Harper's.* She was extremely diligent and conscientious in gathering her material, living with the people whom she described, and participating in their activities, even to marching in a picket line. Her reports were highly informative, although it must be remembered that she was looking for trouble spots, and viewed everything through the eyes of a feminist. She also wrote several books, of which the best-known was *What Eight Million Women Want* (1910), which dealt with the women's club movement of the United States.

In view of her background, the ideas of Mrs. Dorr were surprisingly moderate. Of course she accepted the usual feminist dogma that most social troubles could be credited to a male government that rested on violence, and that if women were given economic and political equality such bad conditions as poverty would disappear; but she generally side-stepped really radical proposals. For a short time she was a Socialist, but changed her position when she came to the conclusion that there was little advantage in transferring power from one class to another. She knew most of the important radicals of the day, but concluded that the usual radical had an ego complex or an inferiority complex, or was "just plain stupid." Her opinion of most feminists was little higher, even though she marched in suffrage parades, and wrote and spoke in favor of woman suffrage. The one suffragist whom she really admired was the energetic Mrs. Pankhurst, whom she called "one of the greatest women that ever lived."[26]

Mrs. Dorr's suggestions for the improvement of women's lot were well within the limits of practicality. She felt that working women could help themselves by organizing unions and by striking, and she herself participated in these activities. She emphasized the passing and enforcement of protective legislation. She felt that prostitution could best be attacked by improving the wages and working conditions of women, but she accepted the importance of such improvements as better schools, parks, gymnasiums, and dance halls. She labeled as ineffective the effort of women to boycott goods made under bad working conditions, but felt great hope for the work of women's clubs. She herself best expressed her own attitude when she wrote: "Woman's place is Home. Her task is homemaking. But Home is not contained within the four walls of an individual home. Home is the community. The city full of people is the Family. The public school is the real Nursery. And badly do the Home and the Family and the Nursery need their mother."[27]

In her later life the future seemed very bright to Mrs. Dorr. As she looked around her, she found the girls healthier, better educated, more sensibly dressed, and with clearer ideas of the world about them. They had increased social and economic freedom, and more and more they expected to have both a career and a home and children. The sexes were becoming more equal in all respects. Mrs. Dorr made these observations in the 1920's, after suffrage had been won and when feminine freedom was a matter of common observation. They showed not only Mrs. Dorr's innate optimism but also the tremendous change that had occurred in the condition of women since the days of Elizabeth Stanton and Susan Anthony.

The ideas of women such as Mrs. Gilman and Mrs. Dorr were increasingly important in the years after 1900, but they little affected the leadership of the NAWSA. The presidents of the NAWSA agreed that women should have greater opportunities and could make greater contributions to civilization, but they continued to follow the well-established tradition that suffrage was the most important immediate goal and that the vote would open the door to other advances. Mrs.

177

Carrie Chapman Catt, one of Miss Anthony's "girls," was president from 1900 to 1904. She was an extremely well-balanced person; as Miss Anthony wrote quite accurately, "She has a marvelously level head!!"[28] Born in 1859 on a farm near Ripon, Wisconsin, as Carrie Clinton Lane, she was an attractive blonde, with a good sense of humor and exceptional mental and physical energy. Her active mind led her to speculate on the ideas of Ingersoll and Darwin, to establish a girls' company for military drill at Iowa State, and to experiment with various life occupations. After reading law she turned to teaching, becoming principal of the high school (1883) and then superintendent of schools at Mason City, Iowa —jobs unusual for a woman. When she married Leo Chapman (1885), she gave up teaching for work on her husband's paper, and at this time she became interested in woman suffrage. After her husband's death she worked on a San Francisco newspaper, and then returned to Mason City. Her biographer holds that her feminism was intensified mainly by the efforts of a man to embrace her, seemingly an unusual basis for ardent feminism. Her second husband, George W. Catt, encouraged her to work full time for suffrage. After her period as president of the NAWSA she turned her attention increasingly to the crusade for world peace.

Mrs. Catt was essentially a moderate, middle-of-the-road person. She opposed many of the more extreme positions of the feminists and especially militant tactics in the suffrage agitation, writing: "I do not, cannot believe that emotion, antagonism, hate, warfare can bring in their wake much that is good."[29] She expected no overnight revolution with the coming of suffrage, and had no desire to fight for other rights, holding that women had plenty of scope for their abilities— particularly since most women would continue to devote their lives primarily to husbands and children. Men could in general be left to run the world, with only periodic suggestions by women as to how to do it better.

Anna Howard Shaw, who was president of NAWSA from 1904 to 1911, was another of Aunt Susan's girls, but considerably more emotional than Carrie Chapman Catt, and Miss Anthony exercised good judgment when she preferred Mrs. Catt as her successor. Though Anna Shaw was born in England in 1847, her family moved to the United States while she was still a small girl, finally settling in Michigan. She remembered her childhood as "very miserable," and insisted that she "never had any girlhood."[30] For some unexplained reason Anna Shaw always wanted to be a minister, with great difficulty finally attended Boston University, and later was ordained. As was even more unusual, she went to the Boston University Medical School and earned a medical diploma. Her interest in feminism increased, and ultimately (1885), inspired by Lucy Stone, she resigned from her two churches to devote her entire energy to winning suffrage for women. Her mighty labors included not only the usual speeches but long lecture trips for the Redpath Agency.

The Reverend Miss Shaw was not a particularly attractive woman. No one called her good-looking, even though her hair, which turned white when she was quite young, was handsome. Her five-foot height seemed even less because she was not only plump but downright fat. Her mental ability apparently was moderate, in spite of her two degrees. Her mind seems to have been slow in reacting;[31] she had little originality and exhibited almost no sense of humor. Intensity of feeling, plus too hard work and a lack of humor, inspired such extreme statements as "I would rather be a free woman in hell than a bond slave in heaven."[32] These same qualities may explain Miss Shaw's periodic descents into deep depression: "I am so tired I feel as if it were all so hopeless. That women themselves love to be slaves and I have worn my best years out, and what good have I done."[33]

The fact that the Reverend Miss Shaw never married admits of various explanations. Her lack of personal physical attractiveness, together with her intensity and her lack of humor, may well have given pause to any male. In addition she exhibited no favorable interest in the opposite sex, her comments being definitely in a critical vein possibly produced by her unhappy girlhood. She felt that the lives of all women had been tragedies and that the real object of Judgment Day "was to give God a chance to apologize."[34] She seems to have distrusted any personal relations between men and women: "It does seem to me that when men & women get together on the sentamental side of life they can become nauciating fools."[35] The rather weird spelling in this statement may itself have significance. Anna Shaw's emotions apparently found their outlet in women's rights and in affection for her own sex. Writing to Harriet Cooper, she addresses her friend by such affectionate terms as "dear heart" and "girlie," weeps over how she has missed her, speculates whether she would still be loved by Harriet if she had to wear a red wig, and pleads that "I want a love letter."[36]

While Mrs. Catt and the Reverend Miss Shaw were extremely dissimilar in personality, they were alike in being second-generation feminists, following paths that had been well located and beaten moderately smooth by the pioneers. Whereas a Mott or a Stanton had been the propagandist of a small group, and had in many ways broken new ground, a Shaw or Catt was following a well-beaten road and was accompanied by millions of like-minded people. Whereas the earlier women had been courageous crusaders for a generally unpopular cause, their twentieth-century successors were primarily executives and diplomats holding together a large movement just on the point of success. These later women were more careful of their words and of their political contacts. Their views were not in any sense unique, or even unusual, and in consequence they have little significance in any study of the backgrounds and characteristics of feminist pioneers.

180

The new spearhead of the woman's rights movement was Miss Alice Paul, who in many ways was more nearly equivalent to Mrs. Stanton than was Mrs. Catt. Born in New Jersey in a Quaker family, Alice Paul had a distinguished academic background, including a Ph.D. degree from the University of Pennsylvania and work in the London School of Economics. Impressed by the tactics of Mrs. Pankhurst, she returned to the United States shortly before World War I with the conviction that the American suffrage movement needed more vigor and aggressiveness in order to be effective. For a time she was chairman of the Congressional Committee of the NAWSA, but still feeling hampered by the conservative tactics and leadership, she formed the National Woman's Party.

Miss Paul was tremendously intelligent, energetic, aggressive, and persuasive; her mind was incisive, and she could make her decisions rapidly and effectively. She attracted as co-workers an able group of women, including Mrs. Alva Vanderbilt, socialite, philanthropist, and financial angel of the party; Mrs. Harriot Stanton Blatch, daughter of Elizabeth Stanton, Vassar graduate, with particular interest in economic matters; Miss Maude Younger, socialite, settlement worker, also concerned with the economic activities of women; Mrs. Inez Milholland Boissevain, Vassar graduate with legal training. These women adopted the policy of opposing the incumbent Democratic Party as a way of putting pressure on it to accept suffrage. They opposed American participation in the war partly because it came when a Democrat was President and partly because they felt any war was destructive and therefore contrary to all womanly instincts. This opposition brought them much hostility in a period of war fervor.

The years after World War I saw the accuracy of a prophecy made by Dr. Anna Shaw to a younger worker just before the suffrage amendment was adopted: "I am sorry for you young women who have to carry on the work in the next ten years, for suffrage was a symbol, and now you have lost your symbol.

181

There is nothing for the women to rally around."[37] The most obvious possibility was training the newly enfranchised women for their voting duties, and the NAWSA gave birth to the League of Women Voters, but the education of voters was a slow and seemingly unending job, with small dramatic values.

Various other ideals were possible as goals for former feminists, world peace being the goal that attracted the greatest interest. Mrs. Catt devoted a large share of her time in this effort. She had joined with Jane Addams in the call which had produced the Woman's Peace Party in 1915; Mrs. Gilman, Dr. Shaw, and other prominent women were involved. This organization was transformed in 1919 into the Women's International League for Peace and Freedom, with Miss Addams as president. The objective was completely admirable and was certainly important to women, but did not have sufficient immediate impact to attract the same kind of support that had gone to suffrage.

During the years after 1920, Miss Alice Paul has remained the real intellectual successor of the pioneer feminists, and particularly of Mrs. Elizabeth Stanton. Miss Paul has worked steadily and diligently for another constitutional amendment, which would provide that "equality of rights under the law shall not be denied or abridged by the United States or by a State on account of sex." This proposal has never been greeted wih general enthusiasm, not only because it apparently would remove protective as well as discriminatory legislation, but because the evils it would eliminate seem small to most people. Women have attained almost unlimited opportunity in every field of life. True, discriminations still linger in particular areas, but the greatest barriers exist in the minds of men and women rather than in legal enactments. Feminism, as it existed during the nineteenth century, has disappeared. Any study of the reasons why women now become feminists has lost all meaning.

10
Why a Feminist

THE WOMEN who devoted their lives to battle for expanding the rights and opportunities of their sex constituted but a small minority of all women. Most women either felt satisfied with their status or were unwilling to express their dissatisfaction audibly. The active feminists possessed traits that set them apart from their sisters, and these exceptional qualities almost always appeared fairly early in life; either they were inherent traits, or they came from early experiences, or both. The exact causes of the unique qualities of the feminists are difficult to determine because of the lack of trustworthy evidence. While most of the women wrote copiously, their comments including many efforts at self-explanation, they were far removed from the events they described, and they had been so deeply involved in the ideology of feminism, that their comments are open to serious questioning.

An analysis of the forces creating feminists is difficult to make, but is well worth the trouble. It should help to clarify the feminist movement itself, but should also do much more, since the conditions that produced one set of social dissenters might have parallels in other protest movements. The nineteenth century was particularly rich in reformers, who ranged from vegetarians to anarchists, and of whom the Abolitionists seemed to be the most hopeful martyrs. Whether the advocates of change were ultimately hailed as heroes or denounced as crackpots they had the common trait of being willing to battle public disapproval in their efforts to produce what they thought would be a better world. The presumption that reformers can be lumped together increases in plausibility with

183

the realization that most reformers embraced more than one route to social utopia. The feminists, for example, were quite catholic in their tastes, with ideas that ramified into almost every conceivable contemporary reform. Possibly there exists something that may be labeled a reform psychology, coming from a limited and identifiable set of circumstances.

Feminism, like other reform movements, was favored by both men and women, and yet the present book concerns only women. The only supportable reasons for limiting the discussion to women are that women seem more interesting because female reformers were less frequent than male, and that whereas the male feminists ordinarily devoted their greatest efforts to something other than feminism, the female proponents gave the subject their major attention.

Women feminists were far from identical in either heredity or environment. They varied in geographical origin, family background, native intelligence, education, religion, marital status, and dozens of other ways. And yet they had certain characteristics that were sufficiently common to seem impressive in view of the almost infinite possibilities of human variation. In fact, an analysis of these women produces something of a recognizable pattern which may well be significant.

The most obvious general characteristic that should strike even the most casual observer is that the women had long lives. From a list of over fifty outstanding feminists, only four died before the age of sixty, and one of these was in her late fifties, while Margaret Fuller was lost in a shipwreck. The number to reach their eighties, and even their nineties, is impressive, Antoinette Brown Blackwell heading the list with a spectacular ninety-six. Long life seems superficially to imply good health and great physical vigor, but this implication collides violently with the claims of almost continual ill-health made by such people as Anthony, Dall, Davis, Fuller, Gilman, and Smith. Possibly these women had troubles which were mainly psychosomatic, since they all lived strenuous lives which seemed to deny the importance of the illnesses that they claimed; but even if they had all been paragons of perfect health, the deducation that physical strength produced feminism would be foolish. The most that can be claimed is that a healthy feminist was more likely to attain national recognition through a life of strenuous activity, than a sickly woman who spent much of her time in bed, and died young.

Geographically, the pioneer feminists concentrated in the Northeastern states, with a scattering toward the West. The few Southern-born women such as Belmont (Alabama) and the Grimkés (South Carolina) spent most of their lives in the North. The almost complete absence of recognized Southern feminists encourages the speculation that the well-advertised Southern male chivalry really existed, and produced happily contented women, but there are more plausible alternate explanations. The early feminist movement was connected intimately with abolition, which made it anathema to almost every Southerner, male or female; any feminist promptly found herself under suspicion as a probable Abolitionist. Moreover, the South idealized the patriarchal family, with both women and slaves as parts of the ideological complex. Interference with the position of either the woman or the Negro was considered a blow at a cherished tradition—an attack on an integral part of a way of life which most Southerners held to be the highest of American culture. This emphasis on tradition remained vital even after the Civil War, when the South was trying frantically and a little desperately to retain at least some vestige of what it felt had been its golden age. Under such conditions feminists had a long and arduous struggle to obtain a foothold in the South.

The feminists almost always came from prosperous, upper middle-class homes, with only a few exceptions such as Farnham, Swisshelm, and Woodhull. Their fathers tended to be lawyers, businessmen, bankers, and ministers, rather than farmers, even though most Americans actually were farmers.

The result was that they were generally urban rather than rural in orientation, though the towns of their origins were frequently very small. An urban, well-to-do home meant that the girl lived a comfortable and even luxurious life, and that her revolt must have been against something other than a poverty-stricken background, although possibly the poorer the background, as with Nichols and Farnham, the more radical the ideas. In a sense, feminism was a byproduct of the Industrial Revolution as the changes gave more favored women a larger measure of time and unexpended energy.

Normally the feminist was well educated in terms of current standards, attending at least a well-known secondary school and, in a surprising number of cases, a college; among the few poorly educated women were Bloomer, Gilman, Swisshelm, and Woodhull. Education had probably little direct effect in producing feminism, since it normally was oriented toward tradition, and almost never included the discussion of dangerous topics of contemporary dispute. Indirectly, the girl may have had her horizons widened, both by observation and by reading. As an intelligent human being with enlarged interests, including work possibilities, she undoubtedly was exasperated frequently by her obvious limitation as compared with boys.

Quite apparent also was the almost universal high mental ability of the women. While the tag "precocious" attached to many of them by their biographers may be viewed with a certain amount of skepticism, their superior mentality seems clearly evident. Any list of fine intelligences would certainly include Anthony, Child, Dickinson, Fuller, Jacobi, Paul, Smith, Swisshelm, and probably many others. Those who went to college were frequently honor students. This mental ability indicates many well-informed and actively questioning women who found difficulty in gearing their minds to the limited interests of domesticity. This statement does not deny the existence of many able women who chose to confine their

186

activities largely to home and family, nor does it imply that all the able women working outside the home were using their talents mainly in battling for women's rights. Just as casual examples, Jane Addams the social worker and Maria Mitchell the eminent astronomer were feminists who spent little of their time in supporting the cause, while Catharine Beecher the educator and Ida Tarbell the writer were not even feminists.

The feminists were intellectually able, but they were not original thinkers, and they were not philosophers who evolved finely spun and closely reasoned theoretic arguments. They preferred to emphasize large abstractions, with stress on the basic "rights" of women as human beings—an application of eighteenth century dogmas. They seldom spent the necessary time to investigate the exact status of women, including the legal, which they continually misstated. When they used specific material, it was for illustrative purposes, and frequently gives the impression of being contrived for a particular purpose, rather than having reality.

Since feminists devoted their lives to the spreading of propaganda, they naturally exaggerated their points, and saw everything as clear blacks and whites; shades of gray were noticeably absent. They continually spoke of their sex as slaves, with no supportable rights, while men in consequence were perforce slave-drivers, plotting to suppress women in every possible way. To carry the argument to a proper conclusion, it must have been men who created the sorry plight of the world, and women would redeem mankind; in this connection, they were generally optimistic, looking for a better world in the future, which seems inevitable if they were to be willing to spend their efforts in reform. Men were pictured generally as selfish, sensual, and bellicose, while women were pious, loving, and coöperative. Only reluctantly and in fits of depression did they admit that men were sometimes desirable people and that women were frequently petty, spiteful, and

187

selfish; their most bitter charge against their own sex was that many of its members were too stupid even to realize they were oppressed. This general attitude had obvious and inherent difficulties. Most of the feminists liked men as individuals and realized that many of their co-workers were male. More important, they really knew, although they hated to admit the fact, that the advance of women depended upon convincing the men.

Exaggerated claims of propaganda led sometimes to contradictions and confusion, particularly when the saving grace of humor was confined to a very few of the feminists. The women talked, wrote, and orated too much to people of their own views, and in consequence tended to become continually more extreme and to discard opposing arguments with no serious consideration. Contradictions were accepted with equanimity. For example, the ladies fluctuated as to whether women were or should be equal with men or superior to them. At times they would argue for equality, then for feminine leadership, and then for feminine dominance. Even the same woman might follow no consistent pattern. A dedicated reformer was completely certain of the value of an extreme goal, not concerned with theoretic inconsistencies. Frequently expressed misgivings, or finely spun arguments to avoid logical inconsistencies, would have decreased notably a woman's effectiveness in the movement and have eliminated her as an outstanding feminist.

The psychological peculiarities and even abnormalities of girls who later became feminists are difficult to state accurately. Several of the women, like Dorr and Gilman, confessed themselves to have been objectionable children, while others, such as Dickinson and Fuller, exhibited early emotional instability. Now and then, as with Dorr, there was obvious reluctance to leave childhood for the problems of adult womanhood. But existing information is too scanty to afford a basis for anything but the most speculative of generalizations.

Whether the women varied from the normal more than any random cross section of the population cannot be estimated with any degree of certainty.

The relations of the potential feminists to their families were of considerable importance unless all current theories of character formation are wrong. A few of the girls, such as Dickinson, were spoiled children. An unusual number belonged to broken families. For possibly 20 per cent of them, one or both parents died while the daughter was still young. Sometimes the remaining parent remarried. In the case of Gilman, the father deserted his family. With any broken family there was at least a reasonable chance that the girl may have acquired a feeling of insecurity, which may have resulted in increased efforts to obtain outside recognition.

The more important parent in terms of emotional involvement was the father, which can be no surprise. Only rarely, as in the case of Olympia Brown, does the mother appear as the dominant influence. Ordinarily the girl idolized her father excessively, with vastly important results whether she retained this hero worship into adult life or was later disillusioned. There is no need to become Freudian to guess that the girl's attitude toward all men, toward sex, and toward marriage was influenced vitally by her attitude toward her father.

Other childhood influences were multitudinous. Many of the women had reform-minded parents, usually abolitionist, and this sympathetic attitude toward reform unquestionably affected the children. Olympia Brown and Harriot Stanton Blatch had the obviously conditioning influence of feministic mothers. Family attitudes toward sex and marriage were also important. The stories of Gilman and Anthony illustrate this point particularly well. In each case excessively rapid child-bearing by the mother left an indelible impression on the daughter, while with Anthony her mother's whole attitude toward sex must have been extremely important. There is a

189

temptation to feel that there were probably many such cases, but quite obviously the necessary documentation is usually absent.

Religion was also related vitally to family background. In most cases the women were strongly religious, although there were exceptions such as Foster, Nichols, and Stanton. Most apparent, and a trifle surprising, was a strong tendency for the women to be connected with the smaller rather than the larger Christian sects. A Catholic feminist such as Nichols was a rarity. Part of the explanation was that Catholic strength was in the wrong parts of the country and among the wrong parts of the population to include many feminists, but also the attitude of the Church toward women was probably a deciding factor, Catholic girls being thoroughly indoctrinated; quite obvious is the fact that Nichols was a late convert. Only small numbers of feminists were attached to the major Protestant sects such as the Presbyterian (Bloomer, Severance, Stanton originally), Methodist (Shaw), Baptist (Jacobi), Episcopal (Belmont, the Grimkés in early life). These faiths apparently cultivated a generally conservative frame of mind; also, of course, their greater geographical concentration was in areas which produced few feminists, and possibly the religion was less important than other factors. Somewhat more usual were the smaller sects such as Congregational (A. Brown, who was later Unitarian, Hooker, Julia Ward Howe); Universalist (O. Brown, Hunt, Livermore); Unitarian (Child, Stone). These denominations tended to concentrate in New England and to be more liberal in their views, both factors of importance. A surprising number of the women became interested in Swedenborgianism, several accepting it as their faith (Fuller, Gilman, Hunt).

The most impressive concentration of women was in the Quaker faith, even though a number of these left or were ejected in time. Among those with Quaker backgrounds were Anthony, Dickinson, Foster, the Grimkés, Mott, Paul, M.

Wright. The near-equality of women among the Friends presumably gave women greater confidence in themselves, while several of the socially unpopular views of the Quakers, as on oath-taking and pacifism, gave the women experience in belonging to a minority that was subject to popular disapproval. Probably most important was the strong abolitionist sentiment among the Quakers, since many of the early feminists started as Abolitionists.

Women fighting for a minority cause might be expected to have had an affinity for other minority causes, but just why the feminists had a leaning toward the occult is by no means clear. Both Stanton and Anthony were strongly attracted to the theosophy of Madame Blavatsky, although neither became a convert. Matilda Joslyn Gage, a close associate of Stanton, prominent in feminine organizations, a co-author of the Stanton history of suffrage, and generally a level-headed woman, went head over heels for numerology; a fascinating, multi-page, handwritten document now at the Women's Archives delves into the subject at length, including the analysis of such matters as the esoteric significance of the stars and stripes of the American flag. Most fascinating of all was the tendency of many feminists to embrace spiritualism. Among those interested were Dall, Davis, Farnham, Foster, S. Grimké, Hooker, Hunt, Livermore, Nichols, Sewall, Walker, and Woodhull. Quite understandable was the attitude of Mrs. Livermore, who became a believer late in life, when she was not very well and was only waiting to be reunited with her beloved and departed husband. For others there was no such obvious explanation, and the reasons for the trend are highly speculative. Possibly the type of mind receptive to feminism also was prone to be impressed by spiritualism, but such a contention is difficult to support by any normal process of reasoning.

After completing their educations, a few women, such as E. O. Smith, got married almost immediately, but the majority engaged in gainful work for a few years before marriage. Favored by a wide margin was teaching, although a few entered other occupations like journalism (Dorr, Swisshelm), the ministry (A. Brown, O. Brown), painting (Gilman), and medicine (Jacobi). One may question whether some of the non-teachers should or should not be in a list of women interested primarily in feminism; if one tried to analyze a list of prominent women who believed in feminism the story would look somewhat different. As for the frequency of teaching, the significance is small except as demonstrating once more such previously discussed factors as good family, intelligence, superior education. But in a negative sense there is considerable importance in the complete absence of future feminists in farm work, in labor in the expanding factories of the day, and in such traditional feminine occupations as housekeeping and the making of dresses and hats. Because of social and economic status these ladies did not seriously consider such jobs, with the result that they were predisposed to a particular point of view. While they now and then mentioned the sad plight of the dressmaker and the mill hand, their real interest was in professional work, and they tended to think of desirable female opportunity in relation to the professions.

The general public opinion of a feminist or other lady reformer was that she was personally unattractive. The *New York Times* expressed this sentiment clearly: "It is a scientific fact that the peculiar species of woman properly known as the female reformer is thin and bony."[1] Testing the accuracy of such a generalization is difficult, since contemporary reactions are often contradictory, and pictures are none too trustworthy. Certain women such as Anthony and Farnham furnished good examples of the *Times* characterization, but they were at once offset by such noticeably plump people as Stanton and Shaw. Some feminists were scrawny and some were fat, with all kinds of intermediate variations. Some were tall, but they

192

were offset by a Bloomer, a Swisshelm, or a Shaw. Some, such as Fuller and Farnham, dressed very badly, but these examples must be weighed against the fashionable impressiveness of a Davis or Hooker. As far as one can judge, the feminists were in appearance a cross-section of the total female population, and in no case can personal appearance be correlated with feminism, with the possible exception of a few girls who thought of themselves as ungainly and homely, regardless of the facts.

The lean and scrawny characterization was a part of the generally popular theory that feminists were embittered old maids who were retaliating on men for the lack of interest by the opposite sex. This assumption is demonstrably incorrect. Practically all of the feminists were married, a good many of them more than once. Of the few spinsters, Dickinson and Anthony clearly attracted sufficient male admiration to have made marriage easily possible if they had been interested. Apparently the one quite intimidating spinster was Sarah Grimké, practically in a class by herself.

The marriages of the feminists did, however, have certain distinctive characteristics. For one thing, they usually came later in life than for most women. In a day when a girl was considered a confirmed spinster by her mid-twenties, a good many feminists did not marry until their late twenties or their thirties. For example, Olympia Brown married at thirty-eight, Matilda Gage at thirty-seven, Stone at thirty-six, Antoinette Brown at thirty, and Jacobi at thirty. The delay was often traceable to feminism, for several of the women started by devoting their lives to a profession or to reform, and felt that marriage would interrupt their careers. Stone was extreme when she promised herself never to marry, but someone like Foster clearly delayed marriage because of her devotion to reform. Possibly also the tendency to delay was related to a considerable difference in age between husband and wife, as with Stanton, Fuller, and Stone.

Explaining the lateness of marriage on the basis of outside interests is not entirely satisfactory, the analysis seeming somewhat inadequate. Even in the mid-nineteenth century marriage was at times combined with a career, while a strong desire for marriage might in any case have overcome conflicting interests. There arises a suspicion that a good many of the women were hesitant about marriage or even hostile to it because of early conditioning. To exclude the effects of early experiences, as with an Anthony or Gilman, seems unreasonable. Some of the women were clearly influenced by girlhood experiences to be apprehensive about sex and marriage, and in some cases this apprehension was expressed in a reluctance to attain physical maturity. The great majority of the women thought of physical sex expression as essentially wicked, their ideal of purity consisting of suppression of any sexual emotions. A few like Hooker were apparently obsessed by sex, but they all were certain that men were more sexually motivated than women and that women in consequence were purer. Such a point of view was traditional in the society in which they lived, but feminists seemed to think more about the subject and to be more deeply impressed than others.

Even beyond the mental turmoil inspired by thoughts of marriage, some of the women held feelings that can only be described as anti-man. While their deprecation of many male traits and accomplishments can be explained as only an argumentative means of advancing women, there remains after reading such material the strong impression that at least in some cases the women really felt hostile to men, or at least fearful of sex experiences. Lillie Devereux Blake wrote at the age of sixteen: "Women have been from time immemorial duped and deceived by men, their feelings trifled with and their hearts broken. This shameful injustice I have determined to redress. I will forget myself and my own feelings in avenging on men their faithlessness. For this men's hearts must be attacked and then trifled with; therefore I give myself heart and soul to making men miserable; if they love me I will refuse them, no matter how much I may be interested. I will live but to redress these terrible wrongs."[2] For the sake of accuracy one must record that the author married at the age of twenty, and then remarried when her first husband died, but her attitude was echoed by many other feminists, and certainly did something to produce later marriages.

Another angle of the anti-man attitude was that the feminists were deeply imbued with most of the current social ideals, even though they were engaged in trying to overturn some of them. The ordinarily accepted attitude was that women were very much superior to men in their kindness, charity, piety, and self-sacrifice. These characteristics were accepted by most feminists as properly descriptive of women, and used as the basis for claiming female superiority. The argument was advanced that women were better in morality and in the worship of God, and that these traits were of dominant importance as civilization improved. Again there is an underlying feeling of sex antagonism which may well have been important in explaining the feminists' reluctance to marry.

The feminists were also distinctive in frequency of divorce and remarriage. Divorcees included Dorr, Swisshelm, Belmont, Gilman, and Nichols. This was a high proportion in relation to the times, and probably indicated a difficulty in marital adjustment traceable to youthful sex and marital orientation. More surprising is the number of feminists who ended with two husbands—for example, Blake, Catt, Davis, Farnham, Gilman, Nichols, Sewall, Woodhull, and M. Wright. The connection of this fact with feminism is obscure except on the obvious basis that the feminists were healthy and may just have outlived the weaker males.

Upon first glance the husbands of the feminists exhibited no remarkable characteristics. They were just what might have been expected of upper middle-class women. Lawyers

195

were high on the list (Blake, Child, Farnham, Stanton, M. Wright), with a considerable number of businessmen (Blake, Davis, M. Gage, Blatch, Mott), a few newspapermen and printers (Bloomer, Nichols), and a scattering of others, such as banker (Severance), minister (Dall, Livermore), artist (Gilman), physician (Jacobi). Only Swisshelm and Lockwood married farmers, which again means only that the women were urban rather than rural in their orientation.

The husbands may have sounded normal in regard to their occupations, but in fact were in most cases a particular kind of man. Many of them were reformers in their own right, as were both Blackwells, Foster, Nichols, Mott, Weld, Stanton. Several of them, like Foster, Nichols, Sewall, Stone, and Weld, were practically as feministically minded as their wives, while others, such as Stanton and Wright, were at least tolerant of their wives' beliefs—sometimes a real test of fortitude as the wife toured the country making speeches while her husband fended for himself. The fact that the ladies talked continually and vigorously of enslaved women's being mistreated by brutish husbands leads to the question of whether their own husbands fitted the generalization. The answer is an emphatic "no," unless one considers certain temperamental differences to be mistreatment. These husbands were not drunkards or wife-beaters. They were usually kindly, generous, hard-working men who loved their wives and treated them well.

Husbands of feminists did not physically mistreat their wives, nor did they subject them to abuse and discourtesy, but there is always the possibility of excessive sexual demands. Here the evidence is limited and tricky. Many of the women were vastly disturbed by the problems of sex, and only Dorr, Woodhull, and Nichols admitted either directly or indirectly to personal sex impulses. Most of them held vigorously that sex was a low passion confined almost exclusively to men, and that pure and sexless wives endured male importunities mere-

196

ly as their wifely duty. They contended that sex expression would be decreased as the higher womanly standards of purity were transmitted to the more earthy sex; Gilman felt that sex would be confined to one short period of the year, as with the lower animals. This attitude suggests that the feminists were unique in having rather little sexual feeling, but this conclusion would be exceedingly dubious. These women were really only expressing the current social ideology, which held that men were the passionate sex and that pure women—which meant almost all women—had no physical passions. The feminists merely accepted the commonly held dogmas of the period, and like other women were probably embarrassed and troubled if they experienced any physical urges; such emotions would create doubt as to whether they were as pure as they should be. Nichols and Woodhull were of course radicals, and not in the best repute with other feminists, while Dorr was a product of the twentieth century, when moral standards changed radically. In general, there is no convincing reason to conclude that the feminists were either lower- or higher-sexed than other women. One can only call them average unless more convincing evidence to the contrary should appear.

The disapproval of sex was reinforced in any wife, including a feminist, by fear of pregnancy. Sex was not only a sin but also a danger. Practically every feminist spoke a little vaguely of the desirability of being able to control her own body, which presumably meant in considerable part the control over childbearing. The modern answer is birth control, but there were several current difficulties. Although the first American birth-control agitation had come in the 1830's, and there was a revival after the Civil War, most women had little or no knowledge of birth-control; at the same time methods used were frequently ineffective, and of course there was a strong belief that interfering with natural processes was immoral. The few women, such as Mrs. Stanton, who referred

197

to birth control were favorable to it; the one exception was Mrs. Gilman, who expected to see sex disappear as an important human emotion.

Changes in traditional marriage practices were often suggested, and were related to the feminists' ideas of sex. Most usual was the insistence on equality between husband and wife, including property and legal rights. Easier divorce was reasonably popular, with Mrs. Stanton most articulate on the subject, although there was some opposition, including especially A. Brown. The critics of feminism argued that easy divorce was really a move toward free love, and pointed to such women as F. Wright, Woodhull, and Nichols, who talked of easy divorce and free love in the same breath, and clearly favored the latter. The feminists replied in hot indignation that they were only trying to eliminate certain human unhappiness and that they expected to lessen rather than to increase sex experimentation; unhappily married people, they contended, were the most prolific source of illicit sexual experiences. Regardless of the correctness of their analysis, the feminists in general tended to be prudish rather than libertarian in their ideas of sex.

The general happiness of the marriages of the feminists is difficult to evaluate. The greater frequency of divorce would seem to raise doubts about it, but such adverse considerations can be offset by citing numerous obviously happy unions. Outside critics tended to picture the married woman fighting for women's rights as an aggressive, masculine, strong-minded person who wanted to wear the pants of the family, and frequently did. This characterization was certainly incorrect, but the average situation is difficult to describe accurately because of a lack both of proper evidence and of a norm against which to check. The result is only fruitless speculation.

Most of the feminists had children, although the average was low because they tended to marry late. Having married when young, Mott had six, Stanton seven, Martha Wright five. Later marriage usually produced fewer—Angelina Grimké Weld had one, Lucy Stone one, Olympia Brown two. Naturally there were exceptions. With a late start, Antoinette Brown still had six children, while Mary Livermore with an earlier start had only two and Bloomer none. But in spite of exceptions, the generalization still holds that later marriage held down the birth rate. All the women insisted that they wanted children and that they loved them very much, and probably they were stating their real feelings, although in view of current public sentiment they could hardly have said anything else.

The feminist laudation of motherhood was omnipresent, but here again the feminists were only expressing an almost universal sentiment. Americans had always worshipped motherhood as the most holy of human experiences and considered a mother a specially inspired person. The magazines were filled with stories and poems glorifying maternal love. Here again the feminists accepted current ideology and then utilized it for their own cause. The superiority of the mother meant the superiority of all women, because all women were at least potential mothers. Motherly traits of love, self-abnegation, service, and piety were the forces that would redeem the world from male egotism, selfishness, cruelty, and use of force. Certainly the feminists had here an argument designed to appeal to almost every American.

Feminists were reformers by definition, and as reformers they tended to view as desirable changes other than the improvement in the position of women. Before the Civil War they quite uniformly supported abolition and temperance. After the war they continued their interest in temperance, which they linked with women's rights. They held that men did the drinking and women did the suffering; the drunken husband was a staple of feminism. The feminists also contended, with considerable evidence, that the liquor interests were the most vigorous and effective opponents of woman suffrage. Frances E. Willard, head of the Women's Christian Temperance Union and most eminent of the temperance advocates, was also a vigorous feminist, and slanted the WCTU in that direction.

The feminists also gave a measure of support to other minority causes, which included mesmerism, phrenology, and criminology. They were concerned with a great variety of social problems, holding generally that more women's rights would eliminate such evils as poverty and prostitution. By the late nineteenth century social work drew increasing feminine attention, and the eminent Jane Addams was an active feminist. International peace had also long been a feminist goal, and greater attention was increasingly devoted to it, particularly after World War I, when Mrs. Catt was extremely active. Such activities were anything but surprising. A reformer in one field had a natural tendency to link his ideas with those of others in different fields.

A contributing factor to the embracing of feminism as a way of life was the desire to attain importance and power. The supporters of women's rights were able and aggressive, with the usual human desire for recognition. In its simplest form, the girl who attracted attention by screaming and beating her heels on the floor grew up to wear bloomers and orate on women's rights. Such an analysis is vastly oversimplified, but when a woman such as Mrs. Davis explained how her work for feminism made her happily conscious of performing social service and of achieving importance in the affairs of the world, one can interpret her statement on a more sophisticated plane. Always there seemed an underlying drive to excel, to show that both the individual and her sex were superior rather than inferior, to justify herself at least to herself, and to produce public evidences of superiority. This attitude showed itself from time to time in the various jealousies that appeared within the movement, and particularly during the split of 1869. The feminist movement constituted an important outlet for the urge toward recognition and power that in another period would have found some other expression.

The present picture of an outstanding feminist is somewhat different from the one presented in the past. The traditional attitude was that feminists were highly intelligent women who were inspired to action entirely by the terrible condition of women, and who devoted their lives unselfishly to assist the millions of unhappy members of their own sex. In the process of developing this generalization the troubles of women have been vastly overstated, the attitudes of both men and women have been misinterpreted, and the psychology of the feminists has been misunderstood. Feminists were highly talented, but they were also real human beings with normal human emotions. Just like others, they were deeply influenced by their environment and particularly by their home surroundings. They had important psychological problems, sometimes greater and sometimes less than those of the average human being. These factors of personality and environment were vital in determining the women's lives, and the very human frailties of the feminists make them more fascinating and even more admirable than the flawless but wooden figures of a poor novel.

Bibliographical Note

AMERICAN FEMINISTS can be understood only in relation to the society of which they were a part. Their characters and points of view have significance in relation to the usual occupations and attitudes of other women. But any analysis from this point of view encounters the obvious difficulties that American women have varied greatly in occupations and beliefs, and that social attitudes have changed radically during the century and a half covered by the present book; to judge a Frances Wright on the same basis as an Anna Shaw would obviously be ridiculous. To obtain the needed background for a study of feminists an intimidating amount of research seems necessary. Included in the desirable reading could be everything written by and about women, which involves an impressive part of all writing. Almost at random could be included intellectual histories, didactic essays, educational treatises, studies of the history of marriage, travel accounts, novels, biographies, and guides to behavior. The largest single collection of pertinent material is the six volumes of *The History of Woman Suffrage*, cited in the notes, and by far the best existing account of the struggle for women's rights is Eleanor Flexner, *Century of Struggle* (Cambridge, 1959), which emphasizes the institutional rather than the personal or social or ideological. Books are of course the beginning rather than the end of research. Newspapers and magazines have almost always devoted attention to women, while manuscript materials are practically unending. The result is that the job of the researcher is impossible unless he recognizes that there comes a time when further reading is unprofitable, and when he can only pray that the thousands of items he has not read will not change the picture significantly.

Concerned specifically with biography are various collections, of which the most accurate and useful is the *Dictionary of American Biography*, which gives sketches of most of the women discussed in the present book. Dr. Edward T. James, under the auspices of Radcliffe College, is at present editing a comparable series under the title of "Notable American Women, 1607-1950." Among the books devoted to group biography are Constance B. Burnett, *Five for Freedom* (New York, 1953)—feminists all; Abbie Graham, *Ladies in Revolt* (New York, 1934); Inez Irwin, *Angels and Amazons* (Garden City, 1933); Lawrence Lader, *The Bold Brahmins* (New York, 1961)—New England abolitionists; Margaret F. Thorp, *Female Persuasion* (New Haven, 1949). An interesting comparison of woman-suffrage and temperance leaders is Janet Z. Giele, "Social Change in the Feminine Role: A Comparison of Woman's Suffrage and Woman's Temperance, 1870-1920," an unpublished Ph. D. thesis in Sociology presented to Radcliffe College in 1961.

Many of the feminists wrote autobiographies. Those of Rheta C. Dorr, Charlotte Perkins Gilman, Harriot Hunt, Mary Putnam Jacobi, and Elizabeth Cady Stanton are cited in the footnotes. Others written by women described in the present book are Olympia Brown, *Acquaintances, Old and New, among Reformers* (n. p., 1911); Eliza W. Farnham, *My Early Days* (New York, 1859); Mary A. Livermore, *The Story of My Life* (Hartford, 1899) and *My Story of the War* (Hartford, 1889); Anna Howard Shaw, *The Story of a Pioneer* (New York, 1915); Jane Grey Swisshelm, *Half a Century* (Chicago, 1880). Unfortunately, several of these autobiographies, such as those of Olympia Brown and Anna Shaw, are not very illuminating about their authors, while at least equally unfortunate is the failure of several of the outstanding feminists, such as Susan B. Anthony and Lucy Stone, to write autobiographies. The autobiographies of such people as Thomas Wentworth Higginson, Thomas L. Nichols, and George Francis Train should be helpful, but in fact are not. Many of the feminists did a good deal of publishing. Those with literary pretensions were obviously prolific; examples are Lydia M. Child, Rheta C. Dorr, Margaret Fuller, Elizabeth Oakes Smith, and Lillie D. Blake. Others who appeared frequently in print included Charlotte Perkins Gilman, Elizabeth Cady Stanton, Victoria Woodhull, Mary A. Livermore, Isabella B. Hooker, Sarah and Angelina Grimké, Mary Gove Nichols, Eliza Farnham, Tennessee Claflin, Susan B. Anthony, Frances Wright, Paulina W. Davis, and Caroline Dall.

Biographies of the most prominent leaders are moderately numerous, but the less eminent women have been largely omitted—probably in considerable part because of a lack of necessary material. Many of the biographies have been written by husbands, by children, by close associates, or by ardent feminists; in these volumes the details may be accurate, but the general picture is colored by natural emotions. Among the biographies not cited in the footnotes are Katharine Anthony, *Susan B. Anthony* (Garden City, 1944); Rheta Childe Dorr, *Susan B. Anthony* (New York, 1928); Alma Lutz, *Susan B. Anthony* (Boston, 1959); Dexter C. Bloomer, *Life and Writings of Amelia Bloomer* (Boston, 1895); Mary G. Peck, *Carrie Chapman Catt* (New York, 1944); Thomas Wentworth Higginson, *Margaret Fuller Ossoli* (Boston, 1884); Mason Wade, *Margaret Fuller, Whetstone of Genius* (New York, 1940) and (ed.) *The Writings of Margaret Fuller* (New York, 1941); Theodore D. Weld, *In Memory: Angelina Grimké Weld* (Boston, 1880); Rhoda Truax, *The Doctors Jacobi* (Boston, 1952)—fictionalized; Lloyd C. M. Hare, *The Greatest American Woman: Lucretia Mott* (New York, 1937); Mary A. Wyman, *Two American Pioneers: Seba Smith and Elizabeth Oakes Smith* (New York, 1927)— literary orientation; Alma Lutz, *Created Equal* (New York, 1940)—Elizabeth C. Stanton; Winifred E. Wise, *Rebel in*

Petticoats (Philadelphia, 1960)—Elizabeth C. Stanton—fictionalized; Alice Stone Blackwell, *Lucy Stone* (Boston, 1930); Elinor P. Hayes, *Morning Star* (New York, 1961)—Lucy Stone; Arthur J. Larsen (ed.), *Crusader and Feminist* (St. Paul, 1934)—Jane G. Swisshelm; Charles M. Snyder, *Dr. Mary Walker* (New York, 1962); Ralph M. Wardle, *Mary Wollstonecraft* (Lawrence, Kan., 1951); Emanie Sachs, *The Terrible Siren* (New York, 1924)—Victoria Woodhull; W. Randall Waterman, *Frances Wright* (New York, 1924). Other biographies with pertinent material include Richard Drinnon, *Rebel in Paradise* (Chicago, 1961)—Emma Goldman; Richard W. Leopold, *Robert Dale Owen* (Cambridge, 1940); Elinor Pancoast and Anne E. Lincoln, *The Incorrigible Idealist* (Bloomington, 1940)—Robert Dale Owen; Yuri Suhl, *Ernestine L. Rose* (New York, 1959); Ralph V. Harlow, *Gerrit Smith* (New York, 1939); Willis Thornton, *The Nine Lives of Citizen Train* (New York, 1948); Benjamin P. Thomas, *Theodore Weld* (New Brunswick, 1950); Mary Earhart, *Frances Willard* (Chicago, 1940); Lydia J. Trowbridge, *Frances Willard of Evanston* (New York, 1938).

Magazines constitute an excellent source for feminism, including its leaders and their writings. Most useful magazine is the *Woman's Journal* (Boston, 1870-1917); its first editors were Mary A. Livermore, Julia Ward Howe, Lucy Stone, William Lloyd Garrison, and T. W. Higginson, with Mrs. Livermore the person really in charge. Several other feminist publications were well known: the *Forerunner* (New York, 1909-1916), with Charlotte Perkins Gilman writing the entire contents; the *Lily* (Seneca Falls, New York, and Mount Vernon, Ohio, 1849-1856?), under Mrs. Amelia Bloomer; the *Revolution* (New York, 1868-1872), edited by Elizabeth Cady Stanton; the *Sibyl* (Middletown, New York, 1856-1864), edited by Lydia Sayer; the *Una* (Providence and Boston, 1853-1855); the *Woman's Column* (Boston, 1888-1924). Nonfeminist women's magazines included notably *Godey's Maga-*

zine and Lady's Book (Philadelphia, 1830-1898); *Peterson's Ladies' National Magazine* (Philadelphia, 1842-1898); the *Ladies' Home Journal* (Philadelphia, 1883-   ); *Good Housekeeping* (Holyoke, 1885-   ). Some help comes from the picture magazines such as *Ballou's Pictorial Drawing-Room Companion* (Boston, 1851-1859), which before 1855 was titled *Gleason's Pictorial Drawing Room Companion*; *Harper's Weekly* (New York, 1857-1916); *Frank Leslie's Illustrated Newspaper* (New York, 1855-1922). Of the more usual and numerous magazines, the most useful are the *Arena* (Boston, 1889-1909); *Arthur's Home Magazine* (Philadelphia, 1852-1898); the *Atlantic Monthly* (Boston, 1857-   ); the *Cosmopolitan* (New York, 1886-1925); *Everybody's Magazine* (New York, 1899-1929); the *Forum* (New York, 1886-1940); *Graham's Magazine* (Philadelphia, 1826-1858); *Harper's Magazine* (New York, 1850-   ); the *Knickerbocker* (New York, 1833-1865); the *Literary Digest* (New York, 1890-1937); the *Nation* (New York, 1865-   ); the *Outlook* (New York, 1870-1935); *Putnam's Magazine* (New York, 1853-1870); *Scribner's Magazine* (New York, 1887-1939).

Manuscript material is widespread but spotty, with a great deal about some of the women and very little about others. Particularly deplorable was the destruction of her correspondence by Elizabeth Cady Stanton. The following collections were used most largely for the present book: American Antiquarian Society—Foster papers; Boston Public Library—Higginson, Weston, and Kate Field collections; Columbia University—Stedman, Gay, Blackwell, and Brander Matthews collections; Cornell Collection of Regional History—Sarah Cooper section of Skilton Family Papers; Houghton Library of Harvard University—T. W. Higginson collection; Huntington Library—Clara B. Colby, Alice Park, Ida Harper, Una Winter, and Anthony collections; Library of Congress—Anthony, Stanton, Olivia B. Hall, and Anna Dickinson collections; Massachusetts Historical Society—Dall collection; New

York Historical Society—Jenney and Dall collections; New York Public Library—Catt, G. Smith, Stanton, Goldman, and E. O. Smith collections; University of Rochester—Anthony collection; Seneca Falls Historical Society—Bloomer collection; Sophia Smith Collection of Smith College—Garrison, Howland, Schain, and Posner collections; Syracuse University —Gerrit Smith collection; Wisconsin Historical Society—Anneke, Ada James, and Stewart collections; Women's Archives of Radcliffe College—Dillon, Olympia Brown, Alma Lutz, Dall, and Jacobi collections. Both the Sophia Smith Collection and the Women's Archives are devoted exclusively to material about women; both are now very useful, and are growing rapidly.

Notes

1. First Stirrings

1. Mary R. Beard, *Woman as Force in History* (New York, 1946), p. 144.
2. *American Museum* (Philadelphia), VI (Nov., 1789), 417.
3. Quoted in Augusta Genevieve Violette, *Economic Feminism in American Literature Prior to 1848* (Orono, Maine, 1925), p. 34.
4. Charles Brockden Brown, *Alcuin: A Dialogue* (New Haven, reprint of 1935); Violette, pp. 38-50; David Lee Clark, *Brockden Brown and the Rights of Women* (Austin, 1922), pp. 29-43; Sidney Herbert Ditzion, *Marriage, Morals, and Sex in America* (New York, 1953), pp. 48-49.
5. L. Mott to E. Gay, May 7, 1858, in Gay Collection, Columbia University.
6. *The Polyanthos* (Boston), IV, enlarged series (Sept., 1814), 298.
7. Mary Wollstonecraft, *A Vindication of the Rights of Woman* (Boston, 1792), p. 92.
8. *Ibid.*, p. 102.
9. *Ibid.*, p. 228.
10. *Ibid.*
11. Robert Dale Owen, *Twenty-seven Years of Autobiography: Threading My Way* (New York, 1874), pp. 296-99.
12. Quoted in Alice J. Perkins and Theresa Wolfson, *Frances Wright, Free Enquirer* (New York, 1939), p. 193.
13. *New York Evening Post*, Oct. 8, 1838.
14. *Morning Courier*, June 10, 1830.
15. *The Diary of Philip Hone, 1828-1851*, ed. Allan Nevins (New York, 1927), I, 10.
16. *Philadelphia Album*, III (July 23, 1828), 60.
17. *Morning Courier*, Oct. 19, 1836.
18. Karl Bernhard, Duke of Saxe Weimar-Eisenach, *Travels through North America, during the Years 1825 and 1826* (Philadelphia, 1828), I, 42.

2. Lady Reformers

1. Mary R. Beard, "Lucretia Mott," in *American Scholar*, II (1933), 5-12.
2. Quoted in Anna Davis Hallowell (ed.), *James and Lucretia Mott* (Boston, 1884), p. 120.
3. Quoted in Otelia Cromwell, *Lucretia Mott* (Cambridge, 1958), p. 125.
4. L. Mott to A. Kelley, March 18, 1839, in Foster Papers, American Antiquarian Society.
5. L. Mott to M. W. Chapman, July 29, 1840, in Weston Collection, New York Public Library.
6. Hallowell, *Mott*, p. 186.

7. Lucretia Mott, *Discourse on Woman* (Philadelphia, 1850).

8. Hallowell, *Mott*, p. 233.

9. Elizabeth Cady Stanton and others, *History of Woman Suffrage* (Rochester, 1881-1922), I, 813.

10. P. Davis to C. Dall, Aug. 23, 1853, Dall Papers, Massachusetts Historical Society.

11. A. Mott to E. Gay, May 7, 1858, Gay Collection, Columbia University.

12. The large collection of the Garrison Papers in the Sophia Smith Collection, Smith College, includes both the marriage certificate and the church letter of disassociation.

13. M. C. Wright to L. Mott, Jan. 29, 1850, in Garrison Papers, Sophia Smith Collection.

14. M. C. Wright to L. Mott, Nov. 17, 1855, in Garrison Papers, Sophia Smith Collection.

15. M. C. Wright to D. Wright, Nov., 1856, in Garrison Papers, Sophia Smith Collection.

16. M. C. Wright to daughter Ellen, March 4, 1857, in Garrison Papers, Sophia Smith Collection.

17. M. C. Wright to daughter Ellen, Oct. 8, 1872, in Garrison Papers, Sophia Smith Collection.

18. E. Stanton to E. McClintock, 1848, in Garrison Papers, Sophia Smith Collection.

19. L. Mott to E. Stanton, Oct. 3, 1848, in Stanton Collection, Library of Congress.

20. M. C. Wright to daughter Ellen, Jan. 9, 1874, in Garrison Papers, Sophia Smith Collection.

21. Quoted in Catherine H. Birney, *The Grimké Sisters* (Boston, 1885), p. 18.

22. Stanton, *Suffrage*, I, 396.

23. S. Grimké to an unknown correspondent, March 18, 1838, in Boston Public Library.

24. Ditzion, *Marriage*, p. 241.

25. The following five paragraphs follow in general Gilbert H. Barnes and Dwight L. Dumond (eds.), *Letters of Theodore Dwight Weld, Angelina Grimké Weld and Sarah Grimké 1822-1844* (New York, 1934); the quotations are from II, 533; II, 533; II, 536; II, 553; II, 640; II, 648.

26. S. Grimké to A. Kelley, June 15, 1838, Foster Papers, American Antiquarian Society.

27. *Ibid.*

28. A. Weld to S. B. Anthony, Sept. 9 (year uncertain), Ida H. Harper Collection, Huntington Library.

29. A. Weston to M. Weston, July 9, 1838, Weston Papers, Boston Public Library.

30. *Lily*, IV (July, 1852), 64.

31. S. Grimké to "Esteemed Friend," Jan. 26 (year uncertain), in Regional Collection No. 97, Cornell University.

32. Stanton, *Suffrage*, I, 354.

33. P. Pillsbury to S. and A. Foster, Jan. 7, 1846, Foster Papers, American Antiquarian Society.

34. The Foster Papers at the American Antiquarian Society contain accounts of these episodes by her daughter, Alla W. Foster.

35. *Woman's Journal*, XI (Nov. 6, 1880), 356.

36. A fine collection of these letters is in the American Antiquarian Society.

37. Pertinent documents are in the Dartmouth Archives.

38. Stephen Symonds Foster, *The Brotherhood of Thieves, or, A True Picture of the American Church and Clergy* (New London, 1843), p. 6.

39. All quotations are from letters in the American Antiquarian Society; their dates are July 30, 1843; Jan. 21, 1845; Nov. 22, 1843; Nov. 22, 1843; 1843; Sept. 11, 1850; Sept. 15, 1846 (?); Sept. 18, 1847; Feb. 20, 1870.

40. *Woman's Journal*, V (Feb. 28, 1874), 68.

3. Elizabeth Cady Stanton

1. E. Stanton to S. Anthony, 1859, in Stanton Collection, Library of Congress.

2. S. Anthony to "My Dear Friend," March 25, 1880, in Dillon Papers, Women's Archives.

3. E. Stanton to M. Lawrence, Nov. 11, 1890, in R. B. Stanton Collection, New York Public Library.

4. See Chapter 8.

5. Elizabeth Cady Stanton, *Eighty Years and More* (New York, 1898), p. 12.

6. Two of the Judge's mourning letters are in the Stanton Collection at the Library of Congress.

7. The following account is based heavily on Stanton, *Eighty Years*, pp. 20-23.

8. E. Stanton to S. Anthony, Sept. 10, 1855, quoted in Theodore Stanton and Harriot Stanton Blatch, *Elizabeth Cady Stanton* (New York, 1922), II, 59-60.

9. Stanton, *Eighty Years*, p. 71.

10. E. Stanton to E. Gay, Nov. 26 (year uncertain), Gay Collection, Columbia University.

11. E. Stanton to G. S. Fitzhough, Dec. 16, 1861, Smith Collection, Syracuse University.

12. See Chapter 2.

13. Lillian O'Connor, *Pioneer Women Orators* (New York, 1954), p. 129.

14. E. Smith to G. Smith, May 8, 1839 (?), Gerrit Smith Collection, Syracuse University.

15. E. Smith to C. Miller, Aug. 23, 1843, Smith Papers, New York Public Library.

16. Mrs. Smith to E. Miller, Jan. 25, 1844, Gerrit Smith Collection, Syracuse University.

17. Bloomer manuscript of about 1850 in Seneca Falls Historical Society.

18. E. Stanton to S. Anthony, in Stanton and Blatch, II, 39.

19. Stanton, *Suffrage*, I, 841.

20. H. Stanton to E. Stanton, Feb. 15, 1851, Stanton Collection, Library of Congress.

21. Stanton and Blatch, II, 30.

22. *Lily*, II (Jan., 1850), 4.

23. E. Stanton to M. Wright, April 22, 1863, Stanton Collection, Library of Congress.

24. E. Stanton to J. G. Whittier, April 11, 1846, Stanton and Blatch, II, 15.

25. E. Stanton to L. Mott, Oct. 22, 1852, Seneca Falls Historical Society.

26. Diary, Dec. 27, 1890, in Stanton and Blatch, II, 270.

27. Stanton, *Suffrage*, I, 861.

28. Speech of 1884 to House Judiciary Committee, in Stanton, *Suffrage*, IV, 42.

29. Diary (see note 26).

30. *Ibid.*

31. Dec. 1, 1872, in Stanton Collection, Library of Congress.

32. *Lily*, IV (April, 1852), 28-29.

33. Stanton and Blatch, II, 49.

34. Lecture of 1876 on "The Subjection of Women," in Stanton Collection, Library of Congress.

35. E. Stanton to S. Anthony, June 14, 1860, Stanton and Blatch, II, 82.

36. *Revolution*, III (April 8, 1869), 218.

37. March 1, 1853, in Stanton and Blatch, II, 48.

38. E. Stanton to an unknown correspondent, Oct. 20 (1880?), Seneca Falls Historical Society.

39. *New York American* as cited in *Literary Digest*, XXV (Nov. 15, 1902), 629.

40. *North American Review*, CLXX (March, 1900), 405-9—"Are Homogeneous Divorce Laws in All the States Desirable?"

41. April 2, 1852, in Stanton and Blatch, II, 41-42.

42. Stanton, *Eighty Years*, p. 43.

43. Ten-page document in Stanton Collection, Library of Congress.

44. *North American Review*, CXL (May, 1885), 389-410.

45. E. Stanton to "Mr. Garrison," Dec. 10 (year uncertain), in Garrison Papers, Sophia Smith Collection.

46. E. Stanton to S. Anthony, Jan. 14, 1878, Stanton Collection, Library of Congress.

47. E. Stanton to H. E. Stanton, April 17, 1880, Stanton Collection, Library of Congress.

48. E. Stanton to S. Anthony, July 4, 1858, Stanton and Blatch, II, 72-73.

49. Stanton, *Suffrage*, IV, xxiv.

50. E. Stanton to O. Brown, 1892 (?) in Olympia Brown Papers, Women's Archives.

51. *Ibid.*, April 26, 1892.

NOTES FOR PAGES 65-79

4. SUSAN BROWNELL ANTHONY

1. Abigail Scott Duniway, *Path Breaking* (Portland, Oregon, 1914), p. 44.
2. S. Anthony to Mrs. Hall, Nov. 15, 1882, Olivia B. Hall Collection, Library of Congress.
3. S. Anthony to E. Stanton, Sept. 29, 1857, Stanton Collection, Library of Congress.
4. S. Anthony to O. Brown, March 11, 1889, Olympia Brown Papers, Women's Archives.
5. S. Anthony to C. Colby, Dec. 18, 1895, Clara Colby Collection, Huntington Library.
6. Anthony Collection, Library of Congress.
7. Ida Husted Harper, *The Life and Work of Susan B. Anthony* (Indianapolis, 1898), I, 29.
8. A. Foster to S. Foster, Sept. 15, 1846 (?), Foster Papers, American Antiquarian Society.
9. S. Anthony to A. Bloomer, July 25 [1880's (?)], Seneca Falls Historical Society.
10. Handwritten speech in Anthony Collection, Library of Congress.
11. S. Anthony to Isabel and Harriet, June 9, 1894, Howard Papers, Sophia Smith Collection.
12. Harper, *Anthony*, I, 52.
13. *Ibid.*, I, 64.
14. C. Catt to L. Anthony, March 23, 1931, Catt Collection, New York Public Library.
15. O'Connor, *Pioneer Women*, p. 35.
16. *Times*, Jan. 22, 1853.
17. *Times*, Sept. 1, 2, 3, 4, 5, 1853.
18. S. Anthony to C. Dall, April 3, 1859, Dall Papers, Massachusetts Historical Society.
19. M. Wright to L. Mott, Oct. 26, 1858, Garrison Papers, Sophia Smith Collection.
20. S. Anthony to F. Anneke, Sept. 27, 1875, Anneke Papers, Wisconsin Historical Society.
21. S. Anthony to M. Wright, June 6, 1856, Garrison Papers, Sophia Smith Collection.
22. S. Anthony to Mrs. Upton, March 14, 1892, University of Rochester.
23. Typed copy of letter from E. Stanton to S. Anthony, Feb. 19, 1854, Stanton Collection, Library of Congress.
24. S. Anthony to O. Brown, Nov. 7, 1867, Olympia Brown Papers, Women's Archives.
25. S. Anthony to O. Brown, July 10, 1868, Olympia Brown Papers, Women's Archives.
26. *Revolution*, I (June 25, 1868), 389.
27. Harper, *Anthony*, I, 169.
28. Stanton, *Suffrage*, V, 623.

213

29. S. Anthony to G. Smith, Aug. 5, 1873, Gerrit Smith Collection, Syracuse University.

30. S. Anthony to E. Stanton, Nov. 5, 1872, Ida Harper Collection, Huntington Library.

31. *Leslie's*, XC (March 3, 1900), 170.

32. *Arena*, XVII (May, 1897), 908.

5. LUCY STONE

1. L. Stone to S. Foster, March 25, 1846, Foster Papers, American Antiquarian Society.

2. Mary Thacher Higginson (ed.), *Letters and Journals of Thomas Wentworth Higginson 1846-1906* (Boston, 1921), p. 59.

3. *Woman's Journal*, XVII (May 1, 1886), 140.

4. Letter of 1850 to E. Stanton, Stanton Collection, Library of Congress.

5. L. Stone to E. Stanton, Aug., 1853, Stanton Collection, Library of Congress.

6. Higginson, *Letters*, p. 63.

7. *Una*, III (June, 1855), 87.

8. Higginson, *Letters*, p. 62.

9. L. Stone to S. Anthony, Aug. 26, 1858, Stanton Collection, Library of Congress.

10. *Sibyl*, II (Feb. 1, 1858), 308.

11. Copy of letter of E. Stanton to I. Hooker, Feb. 3, 1871, Garrison Papers, Sophia Smith Collection.

12. L. Stone to O. Brown, 1867 (?), Olympia Brown Papers, Women's Archives.

13. M. Livermore to O. Brown, April 28, 1868, in Olympia Brown Papers, Women's Archives.

14. P. Davis to G. Smith, Nov. 7, 1869, Gerrit Smith Collection, Syracuse University.

15. S. Anthony letter of no address or date, Olivia B. Hall Collection, Library of Congress.

16. *Harper's Weekly*, XLIX (June 10, 1905), 819.

17. M. Livermore to M. F. Anneke, July 12, 1869, Anneke Collection, Wisconsin Historical Society.

18. M. Livermore to L. Whiting, July 14, 1901, Kate Field Collection, Boston Public Library.

19. L. Stone to T. W. Higginson, Jan. 3, 1873, Higginson Papers, Boston Public Library.

20. Elizabeth Porter Gould, *How I Became a Woman Suffragist* (Chelsea, 1887), n.p.

6. THE LITERARY APPROACH

1. Helen W. Papashvily, *All the Happy Endings* (New York, 1956).

2. L. Child to Mr. Tillinghast, Dec. 10, 1867, Dartmouth Archives.

3. Mrs. D. L. [L. M.] Child, *The History of the Condition of Women, in Various Ages and Nations* (Boston, 1843), II, 267.

4. L. Maria Child, *Letters from New York* (New York, 1844), pp. 245-52.

5. *Godey's Magazine and Lady's Book*, XLVII (July, 1853), 86.

6. L. Child to Garrison, Oct. 28, 1859, Garrison Papers, Sophia Smith Collection.

7. Adolph B. Benson (ed.), *America of the Fifties* (New York, 1924), p. 63.

8. *Love-Letters of Margaret Fuller 1845-1846* (New York, 1903), p. 195.

9. Seth Curtis Beach, *Daughters of the Puritans* (Boston, 1905), p. 196.

10. Margaret Fuller Ossoli, *Woman in the Nineteenth Century* (Boston, 1855), p. 115.

11. *Ibid.*, p. 116.

12. See E. O. Smith Collection in New York Public Library.

13. Manuscript Diary in the same collection.

14. Mary Alice Wyman (ed.), *Selections from the Autobiography of Elizabeth Oakes Smith* (Lewiston, Maine, 1924), p. 43.

15. *Ibid.*, p. 46.

16. Scrapbook, E. O. Smith Collection, New York Public Library.

17. Mrs. E. Oakes Smith, *Woman and Her Needs* (New York, 1851), p. 23.

18. *Ibid.*, p. 20.

7. PROFESSIONAL WOMEN

1. M. Wright to I. Stewart, March 17, 1865 (?), Stewart Papers, Wisconsin Historical Society.

2. E. Blackwell to B. Bodichen, March 25, 1860, Blackwell Collection, Columbia University.

3. This phase of her life is described interestingly in a letter to Gerrit Smith, Dec. 26, 1851, Gerrit Smith Collection, Syracuse University.

4. *Times*, Sept. 8, 1853, p. 4.

5. This and other essays are in Women's Archives.

6. *Woman's Tribune* scrapbook 1885, Clara Colby Collection, Huntington Library.

7. These ideas have been drawn largely from a handwritten article in Women's Archives; it appeared later as "Woman's Place in the Church," in *Monthly Religious Magazine* (Boston), XLII (July, 1869), 26-35.

8. Harriot K. Hunt, *Glances and Glimpses* (Boston, 1856), p. 77.

9. Benson, *America of 'Fifties*, p. 34.

10. *Una*, I (March, 1853), 29-30.

11. *Times*, Feb. 15, 1858, p. 4.

12. Mary P. Jacobi, *Life and Letters of Mary Putnam Jacobi, 1842-1906* (New York, 1925), p. 80.

13. Jacobi Collection, 1894 (?), Women's Archives.

14. Marianne Finch, *An Englishwoman's Experience in America* (London, 1853), pp. 209-13.

15. P. Davis to C. Dall, 1851 (?), Dall Papers, Massachusetts Historical Society.

16. P. Davis to G. Smith, Nov., 1854, G. Smith Collection, Syracuse University.

17. *Una*, 1 (June 1, 1853), 73.

18. Mary S. Gove, *Lectures to Women on Anatomy and Physiology* (New York, 1846), p. 239. ·

19. Thomas L. Nichols, *Journal in Jail* (Buffalo, 1840).

20. T. L. Nichols, M.D., and Mrs. Mary S. Gove Nichols, *Marriage* (New York, 1854), p. 82.

21. Stanton, *Suffrage*, III, 73.

22. Belva A. Lockwood, "The Present Phase of the Woman Question," in *Cosmopolitan*, V (Oct., 1888), 467-70.

8. MAVERICKS

1. M. Wright to L. Mott, July 13, 1846, Garrison Papers, Sophia Smith Collection.

2. Eliza W. Farnham, *Woman and Her Era* (New York, 1864), I, 26.

3. *Ibid.*, II, 7.

4. *Ibid.*

5. *Ibid.*, II, 311.

6. Isabella Beecher Hooker, *Womanhood: Its Sanctities and Fidelities* (Boston, 1874), p. 13.

7. *Ibid.*, p. 95.

8. *Ibid.*, p. 13.

9. S. Anthony to E. Stanton, Sept. 8, 1896, Anthony Collection, Huntington Library.

10. E. Stanton to M. Wright, Dec. 31, 1870 (?), Garrison Papers, Sophia Smith Collection.

11. E. Stanton to A. Brown, June 10, 1873, in Stanton and Blatch, II, 142.

12. I. Hooker, Aug. 28, 1874, O. Brown Papers, Women's Archives.

13. Ditzion, *Marriage*, p. 184.

14. Tennie C. Claflin, *Constitutional Equality* (New York, 1871), p. 33.

15. Theodore Tilton, *Victoria C. Woodhull: A Biographical Sketch* (New York, 1871), p. 35.

16. M. Wright to S. Anthony, April 6, 1871, Garrison Papers, Sophia Smith Collection.

17. Quoted by M. Wright in letter to daughter Ellen, April 19, 1871, Garrison Papers, Sophia Smith Collection.

18. M. Wright to daughter Ellen, Jan. 20, 1872, Garrison Papers, Sophia Smith Collection.

19. *Woman's Journal*, V (July 25, 1874), 238.

20. The following account is taken largely from Giraud Chester, *Embattled Maiden* (New York, 1951).

21. *Ibid.*, p. 66.

9. Changing Emphasis

1. Caroline Healy [later Dall] to M. Choate, 1839, Dall Papers, Massachusetts Historical Society.

2. Caroline Healy to P. Spring, Nov. 30, 1841, Dall Papers, Massachusetts Historical Society.

3. Letter of 1840, Dall Papers, Massachusetts Historical Society.

4. Caroline Healy to Charles Dall, Feb. 2, 1843, Dall Papers, Massachusetts Historical Society.

5. Caroline Healy to T. Parker, June 28, 1842, Dall Papers, Massachusetts Historical Society.

6. Caroline Healy to C. Dall, June 6, 1843, Dall Papers, Massachusetts Historical Society.

7. Letter book, Jan., 1877, Dall Papers, Massachusetts Historical Society.

8. Note of Dec. 5, 1879, in Dall Papers, Massachusetts Historical Society.

9. C. Dall to Anna, Nov. 16, 1852, Dall Papers, Massachusetts Historical Society.

10. S. Anthony to E. Stanton, Nov. 28, 1860, Stanton Collection, Library of Congress.

11. Caroline H. Dall, *Woman's Right to Labor* (Boston, 1860), p. 5.

12. *Ibid.*, p. 62.

13. Mrs. C. H. Dall, "Something about Women," in *Putnam's Magazine*, I, n.s. (June, 1868), 703.

14. Charlotte Perkins Gilman, *The Living of Charlotte Perkins Gilman* (New York, 1935), p. 96.

15. Gilman, *Living*, p. 63.

16. Charlotte Perkins Stetson [Gilman], *Women and Economics* (Boston, 1899), p. 52.

17. Charlotte S. Gilman, "The Model Home," in *Forerunner*, IV (Dec., 1913), 314.

18. Gilman, *Living*, p. 187.

19. *Forerunner*, III (June, 1912), 153.

20. Charlotte Perkins Gilman, *The Man-Made World* (New York, 1911), p. 169.

21. *Ibid.*, p. 152.

22. *Ibid.*, p. 92.

23. Charlotte S. Gilman in Freda Kirchway (ed.), *Our Changing Morality* (New York, 1924), p. 65.

24. Rheta Childe Dorr, *A Woman of Fifty* (New York, 1924), p. 268.

25. *Ibid.*, p. 50.

26. *Ibid.*, p. 263.

27. Rheta Childe Dorr, *What Eight Million Women Want* (Boston, 1910), p. 327.

28. S. Anthony datebook, Sept. 3, 1894, Anthony Collection, Library of Congress.

29. C. Catt to E. Garrison, Aug. 1, 1914, Garrison Papers, Sophia Smith Collection.

30. A. Shaw to H. Cooper, Sept. 4, 1895, Cooper Papers, Cornell University.

31. See entries of Jan. 6, 1894, and May 7, 1894, in S. Anthony datebook, Anthony Collection, Library of Congress.

32. *Times*, I (April 14, 1905), 2.

33. A. Shaw to H. Cooper, April 30, 1896, Cooper Papers, Cornell University.

34. A. Shaw to H. Cooper, Aug. 25, 1895, Cooper Papers, Cornell University.

35. *Ibid.*, Jan. 20, 1896.

36. *Ibid.*, Oct. 8, 1896.

37. Emily N. Blair, "Wanted—A New Feminism," in *Independent Woman*, IX (Dec., 1930), 499.

10. Why a Feminist?

1. *Times*, IV (April 2, 1878), 5.

2. K. D. Blake and M. L. Wallace, *Champion of Women: The Life of Lillie Devereux Blake* (New York, 1943), p. 24.

Index

219

222